The Black Arch

THE PANDORICA OPENS / THE BIG BANG

By Philip Bates

Published June 2020 by Obverse Books

Cover Design © Cody Schell

Text © Philip Bates, 2020

Range Editors: Paul Simpson, Philip Purser-Hallard

Also available

This book is dedicated to my family and friends – to everyone whose story I'm part of.

CONTENTS

OVERVIEW

Serial Title: *The Pandorica Opens / The Big Bang*

Writer: Steven Moffat

Director: Toby Haynes

Original UK Transmission Dates: 19 June 2010 – 26 June 2010

Running Time: *The Pandorica Opens*: 48m 05s

The Big Bang: 53m 41s

UK Viewing Figures: *The Pandorica Opens*: 7.57 million

The Big Bang: 6.7 million

Regular Cast: Matt Smith (The Doctor), Karen Gillan (Amy Pond), Arthur Darvill (Rory Williams)

Recurring Cast: Alex Kingston (River Song), Tony Curran (Vincent), Bill Paterson (Bracewell), Ian McNeice (Winston Churchill), Sophie Okonedo (Liz Ten), Caitlin Blackwood (Amelia)

Guest Cast: Marcus O'Donovan (Claudio), Clive Wood (Commander), Christopher Ryan (Commander Stark), Ruari Mears (Cyber Leader), Paul Kasey (Judoon) , Howard Lee (Doctor Gachet), Barnaby Edwards (Dalek), Simon Fisher Becker (Dorium), Joe Jacobs (Guard), Chrissie Cotterill (Madame Vernet), David Fynn (Marcellus), Susan Vidler (Aunt Sharon), Frances Ashman (Christine), William Pretsell (Dave), Halcro Johnston (Augustus Pond), Karen Westwood (Tabetha Pond), Nicholas Briggs (Dalek voice)

Antagonists: The Alliance

Responses:

'A gripping adventure with plenty of shocks and surprises, leavened with more emotional and humorous material for a heady mix.'

Gavin Fuller, *The Daily Telegraph*

'There are so many questions raised about the logic of how it all fits together, that as soon as you start asking those questions, it really does fall to pieces remarkably quickly.'

J.R. Southall, *Starburst*

SYNOPSIS

The Pandorica Opens

The Doctor and **Amy** arrive in Roman Britain 102 CE, after receiving a message from **River Song**. She shows them a van Gogh painting, 'The Pandorica Opens', depicting an exploding TARDIS, which has reached her via Churchill and Liz Ten. The Doctor deduces that the Pandorica, a mythical prison for the universe's most dangerous prisoner, must be nearby at Stonehenge. The trio find it – as well as a group of Roman legionnaires led by **Rory**, who the Doctor believed had been erased from existence through the crack in the universe[1]. River warns the Doctor that all his enemies are coming for him – Daleks, Cybermen, Sontarans and many more.

The Doctor asks River to bring the TARDIS to Stonehenge and distracts the arriving forces from attacking to buy some time. Amy has found her engagement ring in the Doctor's pocket and queries him about it, but she doesn't recognise Rory when they meet.

The TARDIS takes River to Amy's home in 2010, where she finds two story books, one about Roman Britain, the other about Pandora's Box. She and the Doctor conclude something has been using Amy's memories to set a trap for the Doctor. When River tries to leave, a force takes over the TARDIS and won't let her escape an impending explosion.

The Doctor realises that Rory, and the other Roman soldiers, are Autons, just as the doors of the Pandorica open. The members of the alliance of the Doctor's foes transport down and inform him

---

[1] *The Hungry Earth / Cold Blood* (2010)

11

that all reality is threatened – by him. Despite his protestations that it's the exploding TARDIS that is threatening the universe, they seal him in the Pandorica, as Rory's Auton conditioning kicks in and he shoots Amy... and the TARDIS explodes.

The Big Bang

In 1996, things are very different – just one star burns brightly now, with no others in existence. Young **Amelia Pond** is hoping for someone to mend the crack in her bedroom wall. Her aunt takes her to the National Museum where she sees a petrified Dalek and the Pandorica – which has a note telling her to 'stick around'. After the museum closes, she touches the Pandorica – and it opens to reveal Amy.

Back in 102 CE, Rory is mourning Amy when the Doctor appears, telling him Amy isn't dead. Rory releases a younger Doctor from the Pandorica, and the Time Lord uses River's vortex manipulator to jump between 102 and 1996. Amy is put in the Pandorica to preserve her until she can be restored. Rory stays to guard the Pandorica across the two millennia.

In 1996, the stone Dalek is awakened by the light of the Pandorica but Amelia, Amy and the returning Doctor are saved by Rory. The Doctor hops between 102 and 1996 to ensure everything is on track, but during this, Amelia disappears, and another Doctor appears who apparently dies in front of them. The Doctor works out that the "sun" is actually the exploding TARDIS with River on board, and he uses the vortex manipulator to rescue her.

The Doctor decides to use the restorative light from the Pandorica to reboot the universe but is shot by the Dalek, which is then destroyed by River. He goes back in time to become the Doctor the others saw 'die' and uses the next few minutes to gain access to the Pandorica, making preparations. The only problem is that he will be on the other side of the cracks when the universe reboots.

He survives the crash of the Pandorica into the explosion, but his timeline is unravelling and as he goes, he sees Amy on the *Byzantium* and tells her to remember what he told her when she was seven[2]. When he reaches that point[3], he puts Amelia to bed and tells her about the TARDIS. He then steps through the crack, which disappears.

In 2010, Amy awakens on her wedding day. Initially, she's confused by seeing her parents, and thinks something's missing. At the wedding reception, Rory gives her River's blue TARDIS diary, whose pages are blank. Various items trigger her memories of the Doctor – and the TARDIS materialises. Rory's memories are returned, and the Doctor joins the wedding party.

Afterwards, the Doctor returns the book and vortex manipulator to River, then heads off to a new adventure – with Amy and Rory on board.

---

[2] *The Time of Angels / Flesh and Stone* (2010)
[3] *The Eleventh Hour* (2010)

INTRODUCTION

'We're all stories in the end. Just make it a good one, eh?'

[The Doctor][4]

You and I live in an unimaginably complex system on mind-boggling scales. Consider the universe, an inconceivably large mass full of wondrous things that don't always make sense, a gravitational field stretching out far beyond the limits of even our strongest telescopes. The furthest humanity has physically gone is the moon, an average of 384,400 km (238,855 miles) away from Earth; that's 1.3 light-seconds away. The Hubble telescope has identified a blue supergiant, Icarus, 9 billion light **years** away[5], while the Galaxy SPT0615-JD can be found 13.3 billion light years away[6]. What lies between us and them are stars, planets, moons, asteroids, dark matter, and light across various spectrums.

Consider the universe: it's pretty damn big.

So we cut it down. We relate it to what's quantifiable. We see our own sun, the light pouring through our atmosphere, illuminating the books and trees and animals that populate our little blue planet. Cut it down further, however, and we enter the inconceivably miniscule: an intricate web of photons and quarks and electrons – those ephemeral particles that are all around us, that make up every fibre of our being, but which, when they try to

---

[4] *The Big Bang* (2010).
[5] Gabbatiss, Josh, 'Most Distant Star Ever Seen Spotted By Hubble Telescope 9 Billion Light Years Away.'
[6] Daley, Jason, 'Behold Hubble's Best Image Of A Distant Galaxy Yet.'

teach us about them in school, we often can't quite fully understand.

That's space covered. When we cover time, too, we strip back human endeavours and realise we stand on the shoulders of giants. But humanity's narrative isn't solely made of Shakespeare and Galileo and the Beatles: it's the faces in a crowd, the people we never knew existed. If space and time are connected, we're as removed from, and as linked to, these anonymous people as we are Icarus.

In such a micro- and macro-universe, our comparative smallness can grind even the most grounded down. What's the point of microwave meals, strolls in the park, and comic books if we're just a tiny cog in an immense machine?

Yet it all matters. If you ever doubt that, think of physicists well versed in special relativity and quantum mechanics: they still get annoyed about the queues at petrol stations, wonder what's been added to Netflix this month, and worry that special person doesn't feel the same way they do.

Doctor Who, too, teaches us that it all matters, and that's one reason I love *The Pandorica Opens / The Big Bang* (2010): an intimate tale on epic proportions.

CHAPTER 1: BALANCING THE EPIC AND THE INTIMATE

'Look at this – even worse than his usual rubbish. What's it supposed to be?'

[Madame Vernet][7]

The Pandorica Opens / The Big Bang is a masterpiece of storytelling, bringing very complex concepts to a mainstream audience without condescending or overcomplicating matters. How did showrunner Steven Moffat achieve this? The Series 5 finale is charming and witty and romantic. But it's also an exceptional example of character play, giving viewers a perfect pay-off to the time invested throughout the series.

Structuring the Timelines

Moffat's period as head writer of **Doctor Who** (2010-17) is sometimes criticised for being too complicated[8], a denunciation mainly levelled at subsequent seasons under his stewardship. Nonetheless, Series 5 boasts a prominent arc, interwoven and self-referential storytelling, and is thematically complex. Yet it's commonly listed as one of the show's best[9]. That could be because **Doctor Who** has always pushed the boundaries of what can be achieved in a family drama, becoming more complex in order to

---

[7] *The Pandorica Opens.*
[8] For instance, Cole, Tom, 'Steven Moffat: People Who Call **Sherlock** And **Doctor Who** Too Complex Are "Presumably Fairly Stupid".'
[9] E.g. Jeffery, Morgan, 'All 11 Series Of **Doctor Who** Ranked – From 2005 To 2018.'

cater for such a large demographic range.

Moffat argues that children pay attention to stories more than adults simply because they mean more to them: it's how they understand the world[10]. This is backed up by data showing kids aged four to 15 made up 19 percent of the contemporary audience, and a further nine percent were aged 16 to 25[11].

Our lives are surrounded by stories: we read hardbacks and paperbacks, and listen to audiobooks; we watch stage shows and musicals; we're glued to the television and turn a trip to the cinema into an event. Non-fiction books still have narratives. Dance and opera are bound by plots. Even your anecdotes about holidays, family, and missing the bus involve storytelling. Journalist Christopher Booker noted:

> 'So deep and so instinctive is our need for them that, as small children, we have no sooner learned how to speak than we begin demanding to be told stories, as evidence of an appetite likely to continue to our dying day.'[12]

Fifth Doctor Peter Davison recalled that former Script Editor Douglas Adams 'told me once that the secret of **Doctor Who** is you make it simple enough for the adults to understand, and complicated enough to hold the children's attention.'[13] Similarly,

---

[10] Rampton, James, '**Doctor Who**'s Steven Moffat On Why The Series Is Really A Kids' Programme.'
[11] '**Doctor Who** Exclusive: Matt Smith Is A Hit With Children And Middle Classes'. *Radio Times*, 27 September 2011.
[12] Booker, Christopher, *The Seven Basic Plots: Why We Tell Stories*, p2.
[13] 'It's Never Over With **Doctor Who**'.

Toby Whithouse (writer of *A Town Called Mercy* (2012)) said:

> 'I don't think the problem is that **Doctor Who** has become more complicated, surely it's the fact that the rest of television has become more simplistic... Personally, I think **Doctor Who should** be complicated. Not despite but because it's a children's show. It's fantastic that the next generation of storytellers are being told such rich and dark and intricate stories. When did having to concentrate become mutually exclusive to enjoyment?'[14]

It's fair to say that the Series 5 finale demands your attention. Fortunately, the narrative devices Moffat uses in *The Pandorica Opens / The Big Bang* stop it cracking 'under the weight of too much tangled mythology'[15].

Importantly, the non-linear plot is signposted admirably, using motifs and ideas previously set up in the series. 'All the jumps in time that are happening took us so long to get our heads around, in the most brilliant way,' enthused Arthur Darvill[16]. 'Because it makes so much sense when you've worked it out.'

The Doctor grabbing a fez and mop is a perfect example of this: the early scenes of *The Big Bang* see the Doctor travelling backwards and forwards in time, a potentially confusing notion if it weren't for these motifs acting as visual clues (and light relief). These let the audience later realise when he's about to go backwards to speak to

---

[14] Martin, Dan, 'Has **Doctor Who** Got Too Complicated?'
[15] Robinson, Joanna, 'Can The Man Behind **Sherlock** And **Doctor Who** Be Saved From Himself?'
[16] **Doctor Who Confidential**: *Out of Time*.

Rory in 102 CE. 'We see the same scenes again, or glimpses of them, and we realise what the Doctor was doing each time,' said Moffat[17]. 'He was shoving the mop through the handles of the door as a bolt. And he's realising he then doesn't have a screwdriver.' Once ticking this off, the mop, and, more reluctantly, the fez are both discarded, having established a personal timeline for the Doctor[18].

His differing appearance is slight (certainly in comparison to his adoption of a longer jacket later in Series 6 and costume change in Series 7 to mark the end of the Ponds' era and the start of Clara's), but recognisable enough for the audience to link his escapades in the museum to his escape from the Pandorica. 'And so when you see him acquire those things, you start to get ahead of the game, storytelling wise; you start to think, if you're sat in the audience, "Oh hang on, he's put a fez on now; any minute now, he's going to go back in time and [talk to Rory about being trapped]",' said Moffat, further explaining that he's 'selling a very, very complicated idea as not complicated by allowing the audience to get there first.'[19]

The tension and ridiculousness of the situation are acknowledged by what Moffat calls a 'straightforward farcical comedy' in which

---

[17] *Out of Time.*

[18] Moffat uses the fez similarly in *The Day of the Doctor* (2013); the 11th Doctor is immediately evoked when it's introduced, despite it first appearing in the anniversary episode in a scene with the War Doctor. Once the 10th and 11th Doctors are joined by John Hurt's incarnation, the fez quickly disappears, its narrative function complete.

[19] *Out of Time.*

the Doctor deals with the dangling timely plot threads: zipping between the alternate 1996 and 102CE to save Amy, making sure she's got the sonic screwdriver in her top pocket when the Pandorica opens again, writing the messages that drew Amelia to the Museum, and looking after the six-year-old Amelia[20]. The latter bends the narrative back on itself purely for comedic effect, as Darvill noted: '[The Doctor] gets a drink for Amelia because she says she's thirsty, so he nicks it from her from before, when she had a drink. But the reason why she's thirsty is because she doesn't have a drink because he nicked her drink.'[21]

The situation's seriousness hits home once more, however, when the Doctor from the future appears, only to die. The Doctor concocts a plan to reboot the universe, but the audience and his companions know that he's destined to seemingly be killed. You'd be forgiven for overlooking the obvious question: why would he go back after being exterminated? In retrospect, we know it's to give himself extra time to fix the vortex manipulator into the Pandorica; it also foreshadows him going back in time later on to save himself.

It's a convoluted, twisting chronology, told in a simplified manner using those motifs and by establishing traceable personal timelines for each character.

---

[20] For avoidance of confusion, I will use 'Amelia' to refer to the younger version of the character throughout, and 'Amy' for the adult.

[21] *Out of Time.*

Series 5: It's All Been Leading to This

The Eleventh Hour (2010) does much of the self-referential heavy-lifting; and, since viewing figures unfailingly rise for the first episode of a new era, Moffat could safely gamble that the majority of *The Big Bang*'s audience would have seen *The Eleventh Hour* beforehand[22]. As such, *The Big Bang*'s opening, in which a young Amelia prays to Santa to fix the crack in her wall, directly echoes the first story of the season. Other visual clues show the Doctor's influence on his companions across the series, and so his absence in *The Big Bang* is heavily felt[23].

In the Series 5 opener, as Amelia sleeps on her suitcase waiting for the TARDIS's return, the Doctor's silhouette is seen in her kitchen but his presence isn't explained until *The Big Bang*, in which he picks the sleeping Amelia up from her vigil. In the finale, she has no reason to wait in her garden. The shed he destroys in *The Eleventh Hour* is left undisturbed in *The Big Bang*; and the swing is moved by the rushes of wind which will stir Amelia from her prayer — originally, this was the TARDIS's materialisation. The first shot of both episodes, however, is a close-up of a plastic windmill, repeated to bookend the series and imply the circular nature of this arc[24]. Those trappings remain the same, but the Doctor's

---

[22] As 10.08 million watched the 11th Doctor's debut, and *The Big Bang* attracted 6.7 million viewers, it's fair to say this assumption paid off.

[23] It's similar to *Turn Left* (2008), in which Donna Noble's absence from the events of *The Runaway Bride* (2006) results in the 10th Doctor's death.

[24] Collins, Frank, *The Pandorica Opens: Exploring The Worlds Of The Eleventh Doctor*, p10.

absence fuels the rest of the narrative.

These early scenes are further evoked at the story's conclusion; with life restored, the TARDIS waits in Amy's garden after the wedding, just as it had done in *The Eleventh Hour*, due to whisk Amy off into time and space. By the end of Series 5, Rory's cemented his place in the ship too, Amy actively embracing the event, and therefore the life, she was running away from.

The distinction between Amy and Amelia, ingrained in the show since her introduction, leaves little room for ambiguity when mentioning one or the other: she may still be the same person, but you know exactly which version of the character the Doctor is talking about when he says, 'So tell me, what are we going to do about Amelia?'[25]

A Great Spirit of Adventure

The Pandorica Opens / The Big Bang is a time-travel tale, but Moffat fashions it as a grand adventure – a popular genre more approachable for the general public. The script described the Underhenge as 'like a temple from **Indiana Jones**'[26], and this notion permeates the design, costumes, and direction. The Underhenge set was the largest constructed for the show until that point, and the core cast first experienced it during filming, so they would give accurately impressed reactions[27]. When Smith, Gillan, and Alex

---

[25] *The Big Bang.*
[26] Ainsworth, John, ed, *Doctor Who: The Complete History – Volume 66*, p23.
[27] This method can prove advantageous – like Billie Piper's reaction to the TARDIS in *Rose* (2005) – or the opposite; an initial take for *The Goonies* (1985) had to be reshot after Josh Brolin swore on

Kingston as River Song entered the set, director Toby Haynes – a fan of the Harrison Ford-led franchise – played the stirring score from *Raiders of the Lost Ark* (1981)[28]. It's obviously replaced in the edit by Murray Gold's beautiful music, but it nonetheless added to the thrill of exploration for the actors on set. Moffat described the '10 feet square' Pandorica as 'like a black-varnished puzzle box' with 'intricate, inlaid patterns'[29], its complex otherworldliness akin to the mystical items investigated by the fictional Dr Jones.

Presented with the problem of lighting such an immense set, Haynes suggested the Doctor, Amy, and River use 'movie-style' burning flambeaux (which Amy also uses in an attempt to fend off the one-armed Cyberman looking for fresh meat), often seen in films as characters explore catacombs. And though the huge doors leading into the Pandorica set were partly inspired by those in *The Tomb of the Cybermen* (1967), Haynes credits Steven Spielberg with the ability to inspire awe in actors and audiences, since it's he who 'does those spine-tingling moments really well.'[30]

The obvious point of comparison between the worlds of **Doctor Who** and **Indiana Jones** is River Song, an adventurous archaeologist willing to flaunt rules and who is handy with a gun. However, for *The Pandorica Opens / The Big Bang*, the outfit she wears through much of the story is instead influenced by Han Solo's and Princess Leia's in the **Star Wars** franchise, so she'd resemble a 'female Han

---

seeing the set for the *Inferno*, One-Eyed Willy's ship, at the film's conclusion.

[28] **Doctor Who Confidential**: *Alien Abduction*.
[29] Ainsworth, *Complete History*, p24.
[30] Ainsworth, *Complete History*, p40.

Solo'[31]. Her other costumes, seen briefly at the tale's beginning and end, similarly fit the tone of the period she's in: basic prison attire at Stormcage; a black cat-burglar look when stealing the painting from the Royal Collection; a richly-detailed, opulent dress at the Maldovarium; as Cleopatra in the Romans' camp; and a smart formal ensemble at Amy and Rory's wedding.

Dressed in the hallmarks of an adventure film, the story's beginning feels like a travelogue, and, though it settles around the area of Stonehenge for much of *The Pandorica Opens*, it keeps a solid pace. The narrative starts with a lengthy pre-titles sequence which hops between time-zones and promises pay-off to threads from throughout Series 5. Moffat establishes this run of episodes as one immersive experience, and aims to pay homage to every preceding episode under his stewardship[32]. The Paradigm Daleks return[33], and Rory's death[34] is revisited; Amy's engagement ring, too, symbolises everything she's lost, and is a point of fixation for her since discovering it in the Doctor's pocket in *The Lodger* (2010).

While the stories remain separate and can generally be watched in any order without your viewing pleasure being negatively affected by story arcs, certain scenes and lines of dialogue gain more importance after you've seen how Series 5 concludes.

---

[31] Darvill, Arthur, Karen Gillan, and Toby Haynes, *The Big Bang: In-Vision Commentary*, 2010.

[32] This involved drafting in Andrew Gunn and Jonny Campbell to direct inserts from their respective Series 5 episodes, and writing sequences out of order.

[33] Introduced in *Victory of the Daleks* (2010).

[34] *The Hungry Earth / Cold Blood* (2010).

Most notably, it revisits a scene in *Flesh and Stone* (2010) that many at the time considered a continuity error. The Doctor, having lost his tweed jacket to the Weeping Angels, suddenly has it once more when telling Amy to remember what he told her when she was seven. There's a clever example of wordplay when Amy asks how the crack in her wall could be on the *Byzantium*, and he responds, looking at his younger counterpart, 'I don't know yet, but I'm working it out.' He's referring to the contemporary version of himself, who can be seen checking readings of the crack on his sonic screwdriver; this is also the version contemporary Amy thinks she's talking to. It's only in hindsight that this conversation makes sense in the context of the wider arc.

The series is essentially bookended by playful one-upmanship between the Doctor and Amy. In *The Beast Below* (2010), she saves the Star Whale and cheekily tells the Doctor, 'Gotcha.' In *The Big Bang*, the Doctor plans to save reality when all hope is seemingly lost, and he repeats this sentiment to Amy. It's inconsequential in terms of advancing plot, but deceptively important when it comes to character. Though it's meant whimsically from both parties, it can be read as an affirmation of trust, each acting as the other's safety net.

Changing Faces, Changing Places

Moffat aimed to make *The Pandorica Opens* / *The Big Bang* a sequel to every previous episode in Series 5, and largely achieved this. While all Smith's preceding stories are featured in the clips montage as the Doctor's timeline unravels – and Rossana Calvierri's warning (in *The Vampires of Venice* (2010)) of cracks signalling the end of all things is recalled – the only tale to which it's not a direct sequel is *Amy's Choice* (2010)[35]. Then again, it could be argued that the Doctor is sealed into the Pandorica because the Alliance have seen his dark side; and so have we, in the brilliant but sinister Dream Lord.

That the narrative would pick over the themes of the previous storylines is foreshadowed by the pre-titles sequence. This revisits Vincent Van Gogh, Winston Churchill and Bracewell, and Liz 10[36], and their particular episodes' settings. It also implies the type of narrative to follow, i.e. one boasting a variety of backdrops and ideas, in order to ensure *The Pandorica Opens / The Big Bang* is attention-grabbing.

This isn't merely a matter of changing locales – it's aesthetic juxtaposition, turning a change of locations and/or times from a necessity[37] to a device to keep viewers' attention. It is, of course, an approach common to novels, where interest must be sustained over a greater period: James Joyce's *Ulysses* (1922), for instance, takes place in a single day, but continually moves from one side of Dublin Bay to the other; Arthur Conan Doyle's *A Study in Scarlet* (1887) flashes back from London in 1881 to Utah, 1847; and Naomi Wood's *Mrs Hemingway* (2014) fractures itself between Ernest

---

[35] Ainsworth, *Complete History*, p14.
[36] Respectively from *Vincent and the Doctor*, *Victory of the Daleks*, and *The Beast Below*.
[37] 'In a story involving a quest or travel, small breaks can help pass over uneventful nighttime encampment, for example. We can simply cut to the next morning.' (Kantey, Jordan, 'Writing Scene Breaks And Transitions That Develop Your Story.')

Hemingway's four wives[38].

The technique is often applied to **Doctor Who** to keep things fresh across a multi-part serial. *The Keys of Marinus* (1964) saw changes of setting and genres in each of its six episodes, albeit with the last revisiting the location of the first; *The Chase* (1965) did similar, but further changed time periods; and *The War Games* (1969) weaved various battlefields from Earth's history into one scenario. Further examples include *Inferno* (1970), which shifts the action to a parallel world where a drilling project is more advanced; *Utopia* and *The Sound of Drums* switch from Malcassairo at the end of the universe to contemporary Earth, then *Last of the Time Lords* (all 2007) presents a dystopian version of this world, under the Master's rule[39]; and *A Good Man Goes to War*'s main setting (Demons Run) and tone is entirely at odds with its more frivolous follow-up, *Let's Kill Hitler* (both 2011), set largely in Berlin, 1938.

Perhaps most notable in 20th-century **Doctor Who** for its juxtaposing locales is *The Seeds of Doom* (1976), its use of the Antarctic in the first two episodes contrasting wonderfully with Harrison Chase's lush English country house in the next four. Most impressively, these vistas tie into the story's main topic of an ecological threat, so hold the narrative together beautifully.

Thematic coherency binding unpredictable narratives becomes a

---

[38] Each part further splits between contemporary accounts and flashbacks, so settings include France in 1926, Cuba in 1944, and Idaho in 1961.

[39] *Utopia* and *The Sound of Drums'* differing looks might also be credited to Graeme Harper directing the former and Colin Teague the latter.

key trope during Moffat's time as showrunner. Series 9[40] and 10[41], for example, prominently feature trilogies which casually swap settings while maintaining a sole theme. He even uses this method in longer one-part tales such as *The Day of the Doctor* (2013), which melds together a Zygon invasion in two eras with the seeming destruction of Gallifrey, and *The Husbands of River Song* (2015), moving from the snowy climes of Mendorax Dellora to the luxurious surroundings on the Harmony and Redemption, and Darillium.

The most significant instance of this logic before *The Pandorica Opens* is a tale inexorably linked to the Series 5 finale. *The Time of Angels / Flesh and Stone* moves from futuristic surroundings (the Delirium Archive, and, briefly, the *Byzantium*), to the Maze of the Dead catacombs, then, in its second part, into a forest (via the *Byzantium* again). Its revisiting the coast of Alfava Metraxis gives the tale a sense of symmetry also typical of Moffat's writing; evident from *The Big Bang*'s concluding scene with the TARDIS's dematerialisation from Amy's garden echoing the episode's beginning and *The Eleventh Hour* (2010) – not to mention the way that the Ponds' era is bookended by Amelia's vigil.

However, in *The Pandorica Opens / The Big Bang*, the backdrop transitions are subtle, less surreal, its main change not solely in space but in time (something later used to great effect in Whithouse's *Under the Lake / Before the Flood* (2015)). The

---

[40] *Face the Raven / Heaven Sent / Hell Bent* (2015).
[41] *Extremis / The Pyramid at the End of the World / The Lie of the Land*, and *World Enough and Time / The Doctor Falls / Twice Upon A Time* (all 2017).

location swap even tricked Haynes, who told *Doctor Who Magazine*, 'The set-up for it was great, and I really thought that *The Big Bang* would still be set in the Pandorica chamber, but it just wasn't! It was this massive left turn.'[42]

The Vitality of the Past Enriches the Life of the Present

Each season under Russell T Davies culminated with the Doctor facing the 'returning foe of the series' and tying up plot strands from the 13-episode runs[43]. In *The Eleventh Hour*, Moffat establishes the crack in time as Series 5's arc (quickly reinforced with shots of the crack in *The Beast Below* and *Victory of the Daleks* (2010) before it becomes a major plot point in *Flesh and Stone*). It appeared that this new showrunner intended to continue the traditions set up by Davies.

As *The Pandorica Opens* closes with the much-anticipated cracking of the universe, and the Doctor trapped at the behest of his assembled enemies, the tale would seemingly conclude with the Time Lord repairing the universe[44] while battling the Alliance[45].

But *The Big Bang* subverts these expectations: while Moffat used a child's desire for a dream **Doctor Who** story featuring a 'fantastic

---

[42] Ainsworth, *Complete History*, pp19-20.

[43] The 'Bad Wolf' arc built in Series 1 (with Daleks in the finale); Torchwood was established in Series 2 (and was the basis for the Cybermen and Daleks' battle); Harold Saxon, aka the Master, in Series 3; and the effects of the Daleks' Reality Bomb in Series 4.

[44] Which is what he does.

[45] Which he doesn't do (excepting a determined Dalek).

menagerie of EVERY MONSTER HE HAS EVER FACED'[46] (or as many as practical anyway), the Alliance mainly acts as window dressing[47].

Similarly, a major cast member left at the end of each of Davies' series: Christopher Eccleston, Billie Piper, Freema Agyeman, and Catherine Tate departed across the four seasons and David Tennant left (with Davies) in *The End of Time* (2009-10), the culmination of the 2009 specials. Audiences had come to expect regular departures, and there was no reason *The Big Bang* should be any different. And yet Series 5 is the first 21st-century **Doctor Who** season not to feature the Doctor or one of his companions leaving[48].

In *The Big Bang*, Rory's love and dedication are at the heart of the story's tonal shift. He's separated from the Doctor and (in effect) Amy by nearly 2,000 years. Here's the genius of *The Pandorica Opens / The Big Bang*: Moffat balances the epic and the intimate. A contemporary piece criticised the programme's scale: the Doctor again saves all of existence, and once you reach such heights, small achievements don't feel so important[49]. But this is ignoring a key part of storytelling. Personal tales are just as pivotal as grander ones[50]. After all, the universe is at stake, yet the Doctor is similarly

---

[46] Ainsworth, *Complete History*, p24.

[47] See Jonathan Dennis' *The Black Archive #5: Ghost Light* for more on the programme's self-referencing.

[48] Interestingly, Moffat's **Who** bucks Davies' trend right until Series 9; although it initially seemed as if Clara left in *Death in Heaven* (2014), the mid-credits sequence hints that their story isn't over just yet.

[49] Billen, Andrew, '**Doctor Who** Saves The World, Again. Yawn.'

[50] Such is evident throughout **Doctor Who**. The argument about

concerned about his companions. Amy is the main reason the Doctor uses River's Vortex Manipulator, shifting the action into the future so the Pandorica can take a scan of her living DNA in 1996 and resurrect her. He could potentially have restored the universe using the 'mostly dead' Amy's memories in 102 CE, had he not intended to bring back Tabetha and Augustus Pond too[51].

While the cliffhanger to *The Pandorica Opens* is grand, our last impression isn't solely of every star vanishing from the sky; we're just as troubled over the death of Amy. The scene in which she starts to remember her life with Rory before he is forced to shoot her is as unnerving as the scene it's partnered with: the Doctor, dragged into the Pandorica, surrounded by everything that has ever hated him.

The Doctor is prepared to sacrifice himself to restore the universe – and to make sure his two best friends have a proper life together. This romantic image persists, so the idea that love conquers all is one of the main themes of Series 5 (and throughout the Ponds' time in the TARDIS). Moffat said:

> 'The story of **Doctor Who** is always the story of the companion; it's always their story. It was Rose Tyler's story,

---

scale is neatly summed up by the third Doctor with his 'daisiest daisy' speech in *The Time Monster* (1972) and the Brigadier's summary in the same tale: 'One moment you're talking about the entire universe blowing up, and the next you're going on about tea' (episode 3).

[51] The Doctor's testing Rory in *The Big Bang*; telling him that Amy isn't more important than the whole universe, is, of course, a ruse to make sure his Auton programming isn't still active. It equally tells the audience how much he values the pair of them.

it's Amy Pond's story – the story of the time they knew the Doctor and how that began; how it developed and how it ended... The Doctor's the hero, but they're the main character.'[52]

Companions act as audience identification figures, so *The Big Bang* ends on an upbeat tone. It's that fairy tale happy ending. As the first 21st-century **Doctor Who** to conclude with the complete TARDIS team intact and journeying on together, it makes the future of the show feel unpredictable yet reliable and reassuringly warm. We're safe in the knowledge that there's a good pair of hands at the controls.

---

[52] Jones, Paul, 'Steven Moffat: The Companion Is The Main Character In **Doctor Who**, Not The Doctor.'

CHAPTER 2: MYTHS AND FAIRYTALES

'So, if you're sitting up there in your silly little spaceship with all your silly little guns, and you've got any plans on taking the Pandorica tonight, just remember who's standing in your way. Remember every black day I ever stopped you. And then – **and then** – do the smart thing. Let somebody else try first.'

[The Doctor][53]

Doctor Who frequently explores myths and legends, often finding parallels with alien races: the Minyan race[54] reflected Jason's search for the Golden Fleece; the creature in *The Satan Pit* (2006) and Azal in *The Dæmons* (1971) gave us our concept of the Horned Beast; and the Minotaur in a labyrinth is represented in *The Horns of Nimon* (1979-80) and *The God Complex* (2011). The trend is so prevalent that the 12th Doctor can't believe Robin Hood is his own person, separated entirely from alien intervention, in *Robot of Sherwood* (2014) . Fittingly, these ideas are sometimes revisited[55], adding to the on-going architecture of **Doctor Who**.

Nonetheless, the theme seems to reach a crescendo during the 11th Doctor era. Famously, Steven Moffat described the programme to *The Guardian*: '**Doctor Who** is literally a fairytale. It's not really science fiction. It's not set in space; it's set under your bed. It's at its best when it's related to you, no matter what planet

---

[53] *The Pandorica Opens.*
[54] Seen in *Underworld* (1978).
[55] Leading to three explanations for the disappearance of Atlantis, for instance.

it's set on.'[56] It's no coincidence that Moffat's entire tenure on the show finishes not with 'Once upon a time' but *Twice Upon A Time* (2017); *The Husbands of River Song*, too, concludes with 'Happily Ever After' – notable because Moffat briefly thought it would be his last episode so wanted to give his characters some closure in taking them to Darillium[57].

In her essay, 'Fairy Tales, Nursery Rhymes, and Myths in Steven Moffat's **Doctor Who**', Anne Malewski noted that this period of **Doctor Who** 'continually furthers storytelling via atmospheric fairy-tale references, specific fairy-tale motifs, and general fairy tale structures... These fairy-tale references increase the series' appeal.'[58]

Except, as the 50th anniversary rolled around, the showrunner disagreed with himself. 'I think that most people who are not **Doctor Who** fans, if you described the first four years of **Doctor Who** as a kitchen sink drama would be wondering what the hell was in your kitchen,' he said. 'That's a grotesque exaggeration, and the fairytale approach is a grotesque exaggeration of mine really.'[59]

Moffat credits Piers Wenger as the reason he's quoted as linking

---

[56] McLean, Gareth, 'Steven Moffat: The Man With A Monster Of A Job.'

[57] Reynolds, Andrew, 'Steven Moffat Thought He May Leave **Doctor Who** In 2015.'

[58] Malewski, Anne, 'Fairy Tales, Nursery Rhymes, and Myths in Steven Moffat's **Doctor Who**', in Barr, Jason, and Camille DG Mustachio, eds, *The Language Of Doctor Who: From Shakespeare To Alien Tongues*, pp196-199.

[59] 'Moffat On Matt Smith's Era, Writing The 50th Anniversary And More.'

his tenure on the show with fairytales. In his **Black Archive** on *The Eleventh Hour,* Jon Arnold argues that this is somewhat disingenuous, pointing out that the Series 5 trailer – in which the ground beneath a star-gazing Doctor and Amy rips apart and the pair fall down the resulting hole, only to be faced with a horde of the series' monsters – has deliberate parallels with Lewis Carroll's *Alice's Adventures in Wonderland* (1865). The Doctor also finds Amelia's name enchanting for being 'like a name in a fairytale'; later, 'Amelia' becomes 'Amy' because she deemed her former name 'a bit fairytale'. Arnold consents that Moffat's vision of **Doctor Who** is as a children's show[60]. We can see that from Moffat's *Guardian* interview, in which he continued:

> 'Although [**Doctor Who**] is watched by far more adults than children, there's something fundamental in its DNA that makes it a children's programme and it makes children of everyone who watches it. If you're still a grown up by the end of that opening music, you've not been paying attention.'

(Most pleasingly, Moffat was asked what happens in the Series 5 finale, to which he cheekily, and accurately, responded, 'Practically everything. And some of it twice.'[61])

Certainly our 'way into' the series is through childish imaginations: Amelia prays to Santa because she can hear voices coming from the crack in her wall. *The Big Bang* is significant for not solely recalling these events but reliving them, albeit without the imaginary hero

---

[60] Arnold, Jon, *The Black Archive #19: The Eleventh Hour*, pp61-63.
[61] McLean, 'Steven Moffat: The Man With A Monster Of A Job'.

who falls from the sky to sort out all her problems – in theory. Of course, the Doctor brings with him more problems and doesn't solve the issue of the crack in her wall until the finale, bringing us full circle. That effect is partly achieved through the use of Amelia again, full of wonder and insight beyond her years, probably granted to her **because** that crack exists, making her 'not an ordinary girl' with 'the universe pouring through her dreams every night.'[62]

Even the crack in time arc has its origins in a child's imagination: Moffat saw a similar smile-like crack on the wall in his son's bedroom and wondered if youngsters would conclude something was living inside it.[63] His son, Louis, is also a **Doctor Who** fan, and is credited with giving *Flesh and Stone* its name.[64] In passing on his love of the series, Moffat demonstrates that it's a smart move aiming **Doctor Who** at a youthful generation: 'almost all storytellers strive to make themselves and their stories relevant, and if they succeed, those stories will stick in the minds of their listeners, who may tell these stories later and contribute to the replication of stories that form cultural patterns.'[65] After all, many of the team employed behind the scenes on 21st-century **Doctor Who** grew up with the show and began their professional association with it during the 1990s, when the series was off-air.

---

[62] *The Big Bang.*

[63] Jefferies, Lewis, 'Matt Smith's Debut **Doctor Who** Episode Was Based On Moffat's Childhood Dream.'

[64] Fernandes, Simon, 'Series 5, Episode 5: *Flesh and Stone*.'

[65] Zipes, Jack, *The Irresistible Fairy Tale: The Cultural And Social History Of A Genre*, p5.

This includes Russell T Davies, Paul Cornell, and Gareth Roberts[66] – as well as Steven Moffat himself, who had hoped to contribute to the programme after the success of **Press Gang** (1989-93). But by that time, **Doctor Who** had disappeared from TV. He wrote 'Continuity Errors' for the short story collection, *Decalog 3* (1996) then *The Curse of Fatal Death* (1999) for Comic Relief. Despite being invited to the first Big Finish writers' meeting, Moffat left after learning they couldn't use then-current Doctor, Paul McGann[67] and 'feeling constrained by the past and mistrustful of nostalgia.'[68]

Fortunately, he finally got his chance to script the show: *The Empty Child / The Doctor Dances* (2005) puts a child at the centre of the narrative, albeit as its antagonist, while in *The Girl in the Fireplace* (2006), we first meet Reinette as a young girl, at which point the Doctor essentially becomes her imaginary friend.

It's significant that Series 5 is the only season so far to use a child as the audience's entry point to adventure, an idea intensified by Toby Haynes' direction in *The Big Bang*. The episode's pre-titles sequence is filmed at Amelia's eye-level, a subtle yet important distinction which highlights that this is her world we're inhabiting, and her view that matters. It means the world feels bigger, more uncertain but more amazing[69], and the adults are disconnected

---

[66] Respectively, they wrote *Damaged Goods* (1996), *Human Nature* (1995), and *The Highest Science* (1993), among other titles, for **Doctor Who** novel series in the Wilderness Years.

[67] McGann's Big Finish debut came soon after in *Storm Warning* (2001).

[68] Ainsworth, *Complete History*, p70.

[69] It's used again to great effect for *In the Forest of the Night*

from her life. We hear snatches of dialogue without being privy to the full conversations, enough to inform us that Amelia is both unusual and disregarded by boring old grown-ups.

It's far from patronising, instead placing great value on Amelia. After all, she's the one who believes in stars. Aunt Sharon's worry that she'll grow up to join a star cult ('I don't trust that Richard Dawkins'[70]) is met with a smirk of recognition from the audience and a roll of the eyes by Amelia who sits at the top of the stairs (and whose viewpoint we follow here). This is Moffat and Haynes telling us that children ought to be listened to because their frame of reference is just as important as our own[71].

And that means the world is a scary place too. As Amelia wanders the National Museum at night, the angle we see exhibits from means the polar bears are as scary as the Daleks. What's perfectly ordinary in the daytime takes on a sinister light come the evening. 'I just wanted it to feel massive and eerie for her,' Haynes explained. He achieved Amelia's natural reactions to the exhibition by keeping close to the camera as it followed actor Caitlin Blackwood through the hall and, for each take, called for her to look at different exhibits to elicit spontaneous reactions, 'so that these things come to her in kind of unexpected ways.'[72]

Swiss Jungian psychologist Marie-Louise von Franz believed that all

---

(2014), in which a fish-eye lens at low eye-level shows us Maebh's perspective as she steps into the bigger-than-ever TARDIS.

[70] *The Big Bang.*

[71] It's a message repeated, albeit with less subtlety, in *Orphan 55* (2020).

[72] *Out of Time.*

fairytales are an attempt to describe one field, the Self:

> 'the psychic totality of an individual and also, paradoxically, the regulating centre of the collective unconscious... Different fairy tales give average pictures of different phases of this experience. They sometimes dwell more on the beginning stages, which deal with the experience of the shadow and give only a short sketch of what comes later.'[73]

This seems a fair description of *The Big Bang*, which positions Amelia as central to the plot before giving way to the older, but still somewhat naïve, Amy.

The transition is made when the Pandorica opens to reveal a resurrected Amy, the camera gradually tilting upwards to move from Amelia's point of view to her older self's. Still, Amelia remains a presence, distinct from Amy, so you feel her absence when she's erased from time. Her importance is emphasised further when the Doctor visits her when his timeline unravels, as he realises she's the key to bringing him back.

According to the in-vision commentary for *The Eleventh Hour*, Executive Producer Beth Willis believed that viewers invest in the Doctor and Amelia's relationship because the earliest scenes between the pair were so magical. Smith gives out a warm energy whenever he's around youngsters, which would explain why they play such prominent parts in the 11th Doctor era

It could be that his Doctor has an enthusiasm for the universe that correlates with a sense of wonder found in children. Bruno

---

[73] Franz, Marie-Louise von, *The Interpretation Of Fairy Tales*, p2.

Bettelheim argues that, to an eight-year-old, the elements are alive – the burning sun giving light, the stream exerting its will by flowing, and a stone moving as it rolls; all inhabited by spirits that act like humans, so there's no clear distinction between living things and objects. Empathy blurs the line between animals, so a child 'expects the animal to talk about the things which are really significant to him, as animals do in fairytales, and as the child himself talks to his real or toy animals. A child is convinced that the animal understands and feels with him, even though it does not show it openly.'[74]

Why do we equate storytelling for children with fairytales? The natural answer is that we regale youngsters with fairytales because: i) it's traditional and we're creatures of habit; ii) as such, there's general consensus that they're appropriate for youngsters[75]; and iii) they help children understand the world better. Should we be convinced by the last argument? Surely, the desire to understand the world better is a human trait, no matter your age. Stories form patterns and from those, we infer meanings; arguably, storytelling was born out of aphorisms, an expression greater than itself, an idea with a universal truth. By the second

---

[74] Bettelheim, Bruno, *The Uses Of Enchantment: The Meaning And Importance Of Fairy Tales*, p46.
[75] Moffat agrees that '**Doctor Who**'s quite a sort of positive show, and it's very much connected with children and with your own childhood. It's a world of certainties where kindness and tolerance always work out. So if you're going to cling to a story or fairytale, something like **Doctor Who** is going to fit the bill.'
(Fullerton, Huw, 'Steven Moffat Says **Doctor Who** Is The Perfect Escapism In Troubled Times: "It's A World Of Certainties Where Kindness And Tolerance Always Work Out"'.)

millennium BCE, in Sumer, aphorisms appeared in anthologies linked by themes – 'Honesty', 'Friendship', 'Death' – and circulated around noblemen and priests. These would essentially form guidebooks to humanitarian topics[76].

The Doctor is a fantastical being to children (and certainly to Amelia), but also revels in fairytale adventures[77]. Malewski recalls Bettleheim's suggestion that the repeating of such stories across generations implies parental approval of fantasy: 'thus, the Doctor's love of fairytales, because the Doctor is a figure of authority, validates childhood experiences.'[78]

The main problem with calling **Doctor Who** a fairytale is that the genre is so hard to define accurately. The Cambridge Dictionary defines it as 'a traditional story written for children that usually involves imaginary creatures and magic'[79], which can easily describe much of **Doctor Who**, and indeed, a lot of fiction. 'Magic' is too abstract a term as well: here, it's probably meant as a power to achieve the impossible, but that can apply to many books, TV shows, movies, comics, and audiobooks. Still, many of us can separate the magical happenings of *A Midsummer Night's Dream* and *The Tempest* from the impossibilities in *Hamlet* and *Macbeth*.

Nevertheless, there is a distinction that largely sits in individuals'

---

[76] Shields, David, *Reality Hunger: A Manifesto*, p8.

[77] Look at the way he admonishes Lily for her suggestion that an alien planet is 'Fairy Land' in *The Doctor, the Widow and the Wardrobe* – not because it's a ridiculous concept, but because 'Fairy Land looks completely different.'

[78] Malewski, Anne, 'Fairy Tales', p199.

[79] 'Fairy-tale', The Cambridge Dictionary.

minds. We all recognise the components of a such a plot, including: an ill-intentioned relative or stranger offering the protagonist temptation; abstract 'magic'; a forest[80]; something scary; royalty; and a dream relationship. That's why *Shrek* (2001) and **Once Upon A Time** (2011-18) work. But not all fairy stories have ogres, nor a poisoned apple. Prince Charming misses his cast-call in 'Hansel and Gretel'. The Ugly Duckling doesn't need a glass slipper.

JRR Tolkien attempted to pin the genre down:

> 'The realm of fairy-story is wise and deep and high and filled with many things: all manner of beasts and birds are found there; shoreless seas and stars uncounted; beauty that is an enchantment, and an ever-present peril; both joy and sorrow as sharp as swords. In that realm, a man may, perhaps, count himself fortunate to have wandered, but its very richness and strangeness tie the tongue of a traveller who would report them. And while he is there, it is dangerous for him to ask too many questions, lest the gates should be shut and the keys be lost.'[81]

The notion of a land that's 'wise and deep and high and filled with many things' implies wonder is pivotal to fairytales – something **Doctor Who** definitely excels at. (*The Beast Below*'s opening scene, with Amy drifting in space, underlines this, but the programme finds wonder and delight in the smallest of things: the musical

---

[80] When the world is covered with miraculous woodland, the 12th Doctor tells Clara, 'You remembered the fear and you put it into fairy stories' (*In the Forest of the Night*).

[81] Flieger, Verlyn, and Douglas A Anderson, *Tolkien On Fairy-Stories*, p27.

instrument in Van Statten's museum; singing the blues; and shoes **that fit perfectly!**[82]) Fairytales typically have the trappings of the real world but are exaggerated to include dream-like and nightmare-inducing fabrications. They demonstrate that there is more to see than can ever be seen, more to do than can ever be done, and instil a sense of wonder; as such, the term 'wonder tale' has been suggested as an alternative to 'fairytale'.[83]

The genre implies the invasion of quaint normality by the preposterous and/or dangerous; the importance of travelling, both physically and spiritually; and unanswered questions.

With a checklist of fairytale motifs[84] to hand, we can easily extend many of these to the Series 5 finale. These include:

- 'Cleverness/ trickster/ word games': The Doctor saves himself by affirming the link between the TARDIS and the 'something old, something new, something borrowed, something blue' phrase associated with weddings.

- 'Traveller's tales': The viewer's mind automatically goes to Amy's adventures on the TARDIS, but let's not forget the tales the Lone Centurion could tell.

- 'Origins – where do we come from?': The Doctor reignites reality with Big Bang II.

- 'Human weakness explored (i.e., curiosity, gluttony, pride, laziness, etc.)': Though not human, the Doctor shows many of our frailties; certainly his curiosity has got him into plenty

---

[82] Respectively, *Dalek* (2005), *The Happiness Patrol* (1988), and *Doctor Who* (1996).
[83] Tatar, Maria, *The Cambridge Companion To Fairy Tales*, pp4-5.
[84] Drawn from Gokturk, 'Elements Found In Fairy Tales'.

of trouble, and here draws him into a trap. He appears annoyed at River for graffitiing the oldest cliff-face in the universe, but he's betrayed by his own smirk. Counterpoint this with his reluctance to follow her in *The Time of Angels*, and determination to prove who's boss in *The Impossible Astronaut* (2011) – in both, we know he'll go along with it all anyway, but his pride occasionally trumps his curiosity.

- 'Human strengths glorified (i.e., kindness, generosity, patience, etc.)': Rory displays considerable patience and kindness to Amy, even when she can't remember him. Ultimately, their love for each other overrides his being wiped from time.

- 'Guardians (fairy godmothers, mentors, magical helpers, guides, etc.)': Rory stands sentry outside the Pandorica, guarding Amy and serving penance.

- 'Monsters (dragons, ogres, evil creatures, etc.)': The Alliance, though surprisingly well-intentioned, is made up of ne'er-do-wells.[85]

- 'Sleep (extended sleep, death-like trances)': Amy Pond = Sleeping Beauty. Or Mostly Dead Beauty, anyway.

- 'Impossible tasks (ridiculously mind-numbing, fantastic effort needed to complete, etc.)': All of time and space never happened, according to the Doctor. Saving all of creation after it's already been destroyed is surely the very definition of an impossible task.

- 'Quests': The opening sequence is quite a quest for the viewer, taking us from France in 1890 to Churchill's War

---

[85] The Draconians (from *Frontier in Space* (1973)) were known colloquially as 'dragons'.

Rooms in 1941, then Stormcage and Starship UK in 5145, and the Maldovarium presumably also in 5145, before catching up with the Doctor. Though we don't see much of this sequence, the TARDIS crew travelling on horseback[86] is a clear allusion to traditional adventuring.

- 'Keys, passes (opening new doors)': The TARDIS always acts as a means of progression, in space-time and for character arcs. The Pandorica, too, gets an understandable fanfare when it opens.

The most obvious link to real-life fairytales is the Pandorica itself – based on Amy's favourite story, Pandora's Box. It's shorthand for an easily identifiable artefact, something the audience will recognise without knowing exact details, negating the need for a lengthy explanation. Amy briefly summarises it as a box 'with all the worst things in the world in it'[87]: an overly simplified version of the myth but apt nevertheless. The audience understands the core concept, even if the ins and outs are overlooked.

The Greek myth of Pandora's Box is similar to that of the Book of Genesis – Adam and Eve's expulsion from the Garden of Eden – as well as the Mesopotamian *Epic of Gilgamesh*, specifically the seduction, taming, and integration into civilisation of primitive man, Enkidu, by the sacred temple prostitute, Shamhat (sometimes Šamhat). By exploring temptation and its consequences, it also tries to explain the root of all evils across the world – something which, again, folds back on humanity.

---

[86] Whatever happened to those horses anyway?
[87] *The Pandorica Opens.*

Though we identify it as a Greek myth, Pandora's legend actually derives from an 832-line didactic poem by Hesiod, written around 700 BCE as a way of teaching his brother, Perses, about agriculture, and acting as a moral fable. Set against established ancient Greek lore, Hesiod added Prometheus, the Life Bringer[88] to the pantheon – a trickster who created humanity from clay. Under orders from Zeus, this included a 'fair maiden', Pandora, who is bequeathed gifts from the Gods. Hesiod recounts:

> 'And the goddess bright-eyed Athene girded and clothed her, and the divine Graces and queenly Persuasion put necklaces of gold upon her, and the rich-haired Hours crowned her head with spring flowers. And Pallas Athene bedecked her form with all manners of finery. Also, the Guide, the Slayer of Argus, contrived within her lies and crafty words and a deceitful nature at the will of loud thundering Zeus, and the Herald of the gods put speech in her. And he called this woman Pandora, because all they who dwelt on Olympus gave each a gift, a plague to men who eat bread.'[89]

She's given a large container by Zeus. This 'pithos' was mistranslated by a Dutch scholar named Erasmus as 'pyxis', Latin

---

[88] In the original myth, Prometheus is punished by Zeus for stealing fire from Mount Olympus and giving it to mankind. Prometheus is chained to a rock and his regenerating liver (then believed to be origin of human emotion) is eaten everyday by an eagle. Fortunately, he's saved by Heracles/Hercules. (Or the fourth Doctor according to the strip in DWM 49-50!)

[89] Hesiod, *Works And Days*.

for 'box'. Instead, it was a pot, likely made from metal.[90] Pandora is warned not to open the jar. No prizes for guessing what she does.

Hesiod continues:

> 'But the woman took off the great lid of the jar with her hands and scattered all these and her thought caused sorrow and mischief to men. Only Hope remained there in an unbreakable home within under the rim of the great jar, and did not fly out at the door; for ere that, the lid of the jar stopped her, by the will of Aegis-holding Zeus who gathers the clouds. But the rest, countless plagues, wander amongst men; for earth is full of evils and the sea is full. Of themselves diseases come upon men continually by day and by night, bringing mischief to mortals silently; for wise Zeus took away speech from them. So is there no way to escape the will of Zeus.'[91]

Pandora's Box obviously inspires the name and design of the Pandorica, and from the Alliance's point of view, it would contain the worst thing in the universe: the Doctor. The Alliance act as gods, putting those evils in – although it's doubtful that the Daleks, Slitheen, Hoix, Weevils, and Terileptils would have appreciated the nuances of their own conspiracy and how it links to the ancient Terran tale. We can gather solely that they collated information to use as a trap, not caring for the narrative reasoning.

---

[90] Although some think this pithos, like many other containers from around that period, was earthenware, its description as 'unbreakable' implies otherwise.
[91] Hesiod, *Works And Days*.

If they **had** have checked the story properly, they might have instead connected the Doctor with the 'last hope' remaining inside the box.

In the source material, the presence of hope at the bottom is a curiosity. Some interpreted Hesiod's work as meaning that hope will always remain; others that hope is held by the gods; and others still that hope itself is something bad. After all, why else would it be in a jar containing all the evils of the world?

Nonetheless, in *The Big Bang*, the role of 'hope' is transferred from the Doctor, to Amy, to the remnant particles of the previous universe. It's only through a combination of these three that the universe is adequately (though not fully[92]) restored.

Here, the trio represent 'Chaoskampf', German for 'the struggle against chaos' and an archetype common to mythology. Chaos features in another poem by Hesiod, 'Theogony', which describes the establishment of the Titans. In Hesiod's beginning, there were four entities: Chaos, the state of being before matter; Gaia, aka the Earth; Tartarus, which sits below, and equates to our version of Hell; and Eros, 'the most beautiful among the immortal gods, loosener of limbs, who subdues the mind and prudent counsel in the chests of all gods and of all men.' From Chaos was born Erebus (darkness) and Nyx (the night), and 'from Night, again, were born Aether and Day.'[93] Eros acts as the catalyst for order from chaos (small 'c'), bringing some form of harmony to the four disparate deities and giving rise to Night and Day.

---

[92] See Chapter 3.
[93] Hesiod, 'Theogony'.

It's astounding to see Hesiod's prescience, subsequently building on the origins of the four elements, detailing a battle in which 'Ineffable heat gripped [Chaos]', and ruminating on how a void existed. It's an intangible start with no explanation of where this heat came from, nor how Chaos came to exist. It implies 'temporal infinity', an indeterminate, unfixed origin; a beginning without a beginning, if you will. What we might call circular time would be a notion familiar to Ancient Greeks in their depictions of immortal deities and an afterlife for mortals who have transcended their earthly forms. 'The main object of the first efforts to explain the world remained the description of its growth, from a beginning. They believed that the world arose out from a primal unity, and that this substance was the permanent base of all its being.'[94]

Transitional periods and quests are key tropes of Hesiod's work, perhaps by necessity of epic poetry's grandiose style. *Works and Days* certainly focuses on upheaval and progression, depicting the 'Five Ages of Man'[95]:

1. **The Golden Age**: A peaceful era, in which humans mingled freely with Titans. An endless springtime where no one had to toil or go hungry. Even the dead could roam the Earth. This concluded when Zeus usurped Cronos (sometimes Kronos or Kronus).

2. **The Silver Age**: Zeus gave rise to a period where humanity had to work to live but would first enjoy 100 years of tranquil infancy.

3. **The Bronze Age**: An aeon of war, where warriors would find

---

[94] Fredsvenn, '"Sacred Marriage" Or "Chaoskampf"'.
[95] Gill, NS, 'Hesiod's Five Ages Of Man'.

their punishment in the Underworld.

4. **The Heroic Age**: In this period, humanity were demigods – courageous and intrepid. This time accounts for the poetry of Hesiod's peer, Homer.

5. **The Iron Age**: Hesiod's own time. Humanity had been forsaken by the gods and lived in turmoil.

The latter may seem apathetic; Hesiod might remind you of that bloke who always complains about having to work and blames capitalism for the ills of the world. Yet Hesiod's world wasn't as luxurious as you possibly think. True, around 750 BCE, when Hesiod was believed to be alive, Greece was entering what we now call the 'Archaic Age', which continued for about 250 years, known for its wealth of art and philosophy. Some identify it as the 'Geometric Age', a title derived from the familiar shapes found so frequently on vases from this period.

But Hesiod likely lived through the end of the 'Dark Ages', 1100-750 BCE, when Greeks experienced great political and economic uncertainty. War and subsequent invasions would probably have largely concluded by the time Hesiod lived, but stories of these tumultuous times would no doubt have persisted.

And let's remember that *Works and Days* was a fable for his brother, who Hesiod deemed lazy and dishonest, in order to show him the hidden meanings of art, and how life can be improved through toil. The introduction finds great worth in the structure farming can give to lives (the titular 'works'), includes instructions on the most advantageous times to carry out specific activities (the 'days'), and features, 'perhaps most prominent of all, repeated exhortations always to choose justice over injustice.'[96]

Works and Days was Hesiod telling Perses not to mess up on his farm. Or, 'Life is hard. Deal with it.'

Assessing Hesiod's proposed ages, he seems a dour fellow. The majority of those five periods are depressing, albeit piqued with minor interludes of happiness. His idolising of the Golden Age, i.e. what came before, is in line with the starless universe of *The Big Bang* as Rory essentially lives a forsaken life. The Lone Centurion stays with his dead fiancée, having succumbed to his alien instincts; the universe has collapsed; and he doesn't enquire about what's happened to the Doctor. When the time-displaced Doctor visits him, he doesn't even know the Doctor was trapped in the Pandorica, instead believing (naturally enough) the evidence of his own eyes. He's been utterly abandoned.

Still, there is, as Hesiod states, always hope.

Alongside the Pandorica, hope is also expressed through the characters' relationships, hence the inclusion of Amy and Rory's wedding. One of the main themes during the Ponds' time in the TARDIS is that, even though we go through hard times, love will conquer all. This romantic image of two people who belong together persists (despite Amy and Rory's tempestuous relationship, previously portrayed in tales like *The Time of Angels / Flesh and Stone* and *The Vampires of Venice*). As such, the Doctor acts as their protector.

Tellingly, *Amy's Choice* feels most like a fairytale. Much of the

---

[96] Bartlett, R.C., 'An Introduction To Hesiod's *"Works And Days"'*, *The Review of Politics* Vol. 68, #2.

episode is literally a dream. Upper Leadworth is Rory's dream: Amy's adventurous stage is behind them and they've settled down into a comfortable, quiet existence in the idyllic home they grew up in together. Amy's expecting a child[97] and Rory is an important, highly-regarded, and compassionate member of this little society[98].

The portion in the TARDIS is a definite composite of the Doctor's and Amy's dream – the former at home in his ship, but with danger imminent, and for Amy, travelling with the two men she can't quite choose between, travelling with no horizons. As Graeme Burk and Robert Smith? note, 'In the end, Amy's choice is for both – and neither – options. She opts out of Rory's dream, out of a boring existence in a picturesque village to be in the TARDIS with the Doctor, but she also chooses to be with Rory in that reality.'[99]

Leadworth consists of a spacious village green, a pub and a post office, and locals who all appear to know each other[100]. This rural setting is far removed from the environs of the Russell T Davies years; it feels distinctly like something from 20th-century **Doctor Who**, reminiscent of *The Dæmons*, *The Android Invasion* (1975),

---

[97] This gains extra importance after viewing *Asylum of the Daleks* (2012), in which Amy tells us that Rory's always wanted kids.
[98] Could the idea of Upper Leadworth also appeal to the Doctor? An ordinary life seems both miraculous and a terrible nightmare to him. However, his constant putdowns ('what do you do around here to stave off the, you know, self-harm?') perhaps belie his wish to see the Ponds out of harm's way.
[99] Burk, Graeme, and Robert Smith?, *Who Is The Doctor: The Unofficial Guide To Doctor Who*, p312.
[100] So much so that Mrs Angelo and Jeff are not only on first-name terms with Amy but also know about her imaginary friend, the Doctor.

and *The Awakening* (1984). It initially appears as a decision to differentiate from what **Doctor Who** had been serving up in the previous four series, and to leave the Doctor relying solely on his wits to find Prisoner Zero and defeat the Atraxi in *The Eleventh Hour*. However, Series 5 returns to Leadworth (and Upper Leadworth), further takes in quaint Welsh village Cwmtaff, and makes even cities cosy by focusing on familial aspects and concerns[101].

The Big Bang cements Amy and Rory's relationship: even though Rory shoots his own fiancée, he redeems himself by guarding her for approximately 2,000 years. 'I think that's just the ultimate romantic gesture, I suppose,' Karen Gillan said. 'It kind of just shows how much he actually loves Amy and when she finds that out, I think she realises how much she loves him. And it's kind of the perfect end to a love story.'[102]

It's particularly pleasing that *The Big Bang* goes off in an unexpected direction: while the viewer might be expecting a grand conflict, the crux of the matter is more personal. That's endemic of how the narrative largely subverts fairytale and mythic expectations.

---

[101] The school in *The Vampires of Venice* is sinister yet symbolises our natural instincts to look after one's own; this is further demonstrated by Guido's desperation to save his daughter, Isabella, from said school. Colchester's technically a town, not a city, but it's shown in *The Lodger* as an intimate place because we don't leave the confines of Craig's house for very long – and when we do, it's to visit the park.
[102] *Out of Time.*

Notably, the Pandorica isn't what everyone thinks it is. The episode focuses on the box, but it's actually Pandora (i.e. Amy) who poses the real threat. The box purports to contain something terrible, but instead, contains nothing material until the Alliance put in the one person we identify as a saviour. Then, when it's opened again at the start of *The Big Bang*, the rug is pulled from underneath us when we find Amy in there in place of the Doctor. She's revived by the Doctor's actions, yes, but it's her troubled childhood that's the catalyst for her healing: 'the men keep watch and help her, but she is her own salvation: her childhood, source of pain and anguish and trauma, comes to the rescue of the adult, strong woman she has become.'[103]

Nonetheless, Amelia demonstrates great independence and trust in otherworldliness when she hides from her Aunt Sharon in the museum – a decision she makes solely through an attachment to the idea of something greater and more mysterious than disappointing reality. She's the girl who imagines stars. The relationship between Amy and Amelia illustrates how what goes on in our youth affects our older selves.

Amy has enjoyed time journeying into space and time, but there's not such a great gulf between her and Amelia.

Amy has represented temptation previously in the series, prominently in *Flesh and Stone*, and she provides the temptation in the finale too, her personality used to devise a scenario to ensnare the Doctor. But she's more than that. Her memories are the means

---

[103] Maleski, Sam, 'Tiberian Thoughts: The Woman And The Trap – **Who** and the Myth of Pandora.'

of the universe's return; far from Pandora, who's been manipulated and seemingly doesn't undo the wrong her opening the box has wrought, Amy provides the solution too. The parallel with **The Sarah Jane Adventures** (2007-11) episode, *Death of the Doctor* (2010), is uncanny – and especially telling that it's the next TV story chronologically after *The Big Bang*. 'The coffin was the trap; the coffin was the solution,' says the Doctor then. 'That's so neat, I could write a thesis.'[104]

Nonetheless, the audience should have guessed that events wouldn't proceed in the expected way, when the Doctor describes the being trapped in the Pandorica:

> 'There was a goblin or a trickster or a warrior. A nameless, terrible thing, soaked in the blood of a billion galaxies. The most feared being in all the cosmos. And nothing could stop it, or hold it, or reason with it. One day, it would just drop out of the sky and tear down your world.'[105]

It's a chilling summary of our Time Lord, but entirely suitable, especially if you approach it from the point of view of the Alliance. To them, he **is** a warrior, soaked in their blood. The Great Intelligence points out as much in *The Name of the Doctor* (2013), asking what 'the leader of the Sycorax[106], or Solomon the trader[107], or the Cybermen, or the Daleks' would make of Vastra's claim otherwise. These descriptions become more relevant after *A Good Man Goes To War*, where the title 'Doctor' means 'mighty warrior'

---

[104] **The Sarah Jane Adventures**: *Death of the Doctor* episode 2.
[105] *The Pandorica Opens.*
[106] *The Christmas Invasion* (2005).
[107] *Dinosaurs on a Spaceship* (2012).

56

to the people of the Gamma Forests. That the Doctor is 'nameless' becomes increasingly significant throughout the 11th Doctor's reign, as the oldest question in the universe is revealed to be 'Doctor who?'

The idea of the Time Lord dropping out of the sky and tearing down your world is obvious, and while we may balk at the assertion that nothing could 'reason with it' – seeing as the Doctor frequently gives enemies a choice or a chance – it's not that outlandish. Look at *The Lie of the Land* (2017) for an example of how the Doctor's morality is seen by others as skewed. 'Your version of good is not absolute,' Missy notes, cuttingly. 'It's vain, arrogant, and sentimental.' The Daleks, for instance, genuinely believe they're doing right by exterminating 'lesser' races[108]; the Cybermen, too, work to upgrade humanity by getting rid of our frailties.

There's a further neat subversion in the Pandorica legend when River notes, 'I hate good wizards in fairytales. They always turn out to be [the Doctor].'[109] The image of the Doctor as a wizard surely brings to mind *Battlefield* (1989), in which the seventh Doctor is mistaken for Merlin, a role he's professedly played in another universe. Whether we interpret 'good' as 'the opposite of evil' or 'particularly adept' doesn't matter – the deception is so clever because it's plain for all to see. This is, after all, a story by Steven

---

[108] Or at least, that's what the Doctor believes. In *Dalek* (2005), Van Statten asks why the lone Dalek would murder the nearby population of Salt Lake City, and beyond. The ninth Doctor explains, 'Because it honestly believes they should die. Human beings are different, and anything different is wrong.'
[109] *The Pandorica Opens.*

Moffat: you know it's not going to go as planned.

The Pandorica Opens / The Big Bang works because it debases standard mythological structure... or does it? The distinction between good and evil is blurred in *The Pandorica Opens*. We consider the goods and evils in myths and fairytales as polar opposites. The wolf is bad; Little Red Riding Hood is good. Except the wolf is simply hungry. That doesn't necessarily make it bad – or if it does, it's only as bad as you or I.

The Doctor is described as a trickster, but if we once more consult that aforementioned list of fairytale motifs, the term is listed as 'sometimes a hero, sometimes on the side of evil but humans benefit'.[110] Indeed, Prometheus was a trickster from the pantheon's perspective, yet, according to Hesiod's *Works and Days*, we should be thankful for his trickery which resulted in his creating humanity.

The Doctor, then, treads the line between good and evil. Where he falls is a matter of opinion. In some ways, he's a hybrid. In others, he's an anomaly, an especially fine summation of the roles he plays in the Series 5 conclusion.

---

[110] Gokturk, 'Elements'.

CHAPTER 3: ANOMALIES

'If something can be remembered, it can come back.'

[The Doctor][111]

Steven Moffat's writing is, if not always nostalgic, then certainly idealistic. With Leadworth, he gives us a picturesque English village; through the Doctor's companions, we see true dedication and love; and in the plot as a whole, there's the need for wrongs to be righted, for goodness to prevail, and for explanations (largely) to be forthcoming. The central idea of Series 5 might be the importance of memory.

And so, we're teased with timely anomalies that hint at what we've lost and what could return.

We come across anomalies – that is, a deviation from the norm – now and then. Test results might pick up abnormalities in an organism; statistics show what the average person does in a situation but cannot accurately predict outliers; and geographical irregularities are typically disputed areas of land.

Doctor Who boasts different forms of anomalies, but the show is chiefly about two in particular: the Doctor and the TARDIS. These abnormalities don't make a great deal of sense, principally because they travel through time and their origins are unknown (but, in the TARDIS's case, also due to its dimensional transcendentalism).

For *The Pandorica Opens / The Big Bang*, anomalies are things that simply cannot exist and yet do. The latter episode is full of them,

---

[111] *The Pandorica Opens.*

because it largely takes place in an altered timeline in which Total Event Collapse has occurred.

Presented in the National Museum, the Pandorica adopts a new name: 'The Anomaly'. In what way is that an accurate description? Sat at the heart of the Museum, this monolith is described as: 'THE PANDORICA, THE INEXPLICABLE, LEGENDARY PUZZLE BOX – A MYSTERY SPANNING THOUSANDS OF YEARS.' From humanity's perspective, it's existed since at least Roman times[112], unblemished. Its intricacies seem an impossibility for the time in which it would have been constructed. It's equivalent to our questioning how the Egyptians could create the Pyramids – or indeed how 'early man' could construct Stonehenge[113].

Therefore, humanity would have inferred that the Pandorica was constructed on Earth, by *Homo sapiens* (lacking much evidence of other intelligent life[114]), at a time humans simply **couldn't** have created it.

Presumably, the Pandorica is impervious to scans on different spectrums; otherwise, at some stage, there would have been a

---

[112] Stonehenge was, in 102 CE, already old. The stones' 'roots' extend down to the Underhenge, so we don't actually know how long the Pandorica has been there, nor how the Alliance knows when the TARDIS arrives. Presumably, it's a fixed point, similar to the Doctor's supposed death at Lake Silencio on 22 April 2011; if we go by Vincent's painting, the space-time co-ordinates indicate a set period, so the Alliance made the Pandorica with plenty of time to spare.

[113] *The Time Meddler* (1965) suggests it was constructed using the Monk's anti-gravity lifts.

[114] With some exceptions, which we'll come back to.

concerted effort to rescue the person seated inside. Going against the Doctor's argument that 'anyone can break into a prison'[115], it doesn't appear that humans could manage this feat. Maybe this is because the Pandorica recognises that someone is inside, so refuses to let anyone else enter – that is, after all, its purpose. After the Doctor is sealed inside, Rory opens it with the sonic screwdriver; then when Amy's inside, the Pandorica presumably detects a further anomaly in the shape of Amelia – the same person both inside and outside the box. In an early draft of the script, we're shown a point-of-view shot from inside the Pandorica of the Doctor's handprint touching the outside; this is then scanned and analysed, which means the Box can recognise certain individuals and react accordingly[116].

It was also guarded by the Last Centurion, a figure who's stood as its protector for nearly 2,000 years, only disappearing in the Second World War. They're an anomalous pairing, two ageless, indefinable things.

The Pandorica's original setting, Stonehenge, adds to the anomalous situation:

> 'Beside the main group [of monoliths] stands a large solitary stone. Each year on about 22 June, in the morning, a person standing in the middle of the circle can see the sun rise directly behind the large single stone, a phenomenon which has led some people to believe that the monument was

---

[115] *The Pandorica Opens.*
[116] Ainsworth, *Complete History*, p24.

dedicated to the sun.'[117]

It's ironic, then, that Stonehenge finally makes its proper **Doctor Who** debut in a story which eliminates our own star[118].

Except it's not just the Pandorica that's an anomaly in the museum; there's an argument to be made that 'The Anomaly' refers not simply to the box, but to a wider exhibition of which the Pandorica is the centrepiece. 'One of the consequences of the elimination of all reality is that a lot of the history of Earth at that point of course will make absolutely no sense,' explained Moffat before giving an example of the remnants from the previous universe: 'There'll presumably be observatories, but no stars to look at.'[119]

In the museum, Amelia treads a path through a collection of spooky objects.

'POLAR BEARS IN AUSTRALIA

'LOCAL AUSTRALIAN PUNTERS HAVE SPOTTED LARGE WHITE BEARS AT DIFFERENT POINTS ALONG THE OUT BACK.

'They can't exist and yet they do.'

That last line becomes something of a mantra for the exhibition, appearing alongside the Nile penguins, Pharaohs of the Himalayas, and the Daleks. In all these instances, we have beings in surroundings we don't associate them with, and two of these examples have chilling parallels to reality.

---

[117] Verdet, Jean-Pierre, and Anthony Zielonka, *The Sky: Order And Chaos*, p12.
[118] It's briefly seen in *Doctor Who* (1996) before this.
[119] *Out of Time*.

Polar bears roam the Arctic, their bodies insulated by thick fur that even covers their large feet. Underneath, their skin is black, enabling them to soak up sunlight more easily. They're obviously not adapted for hotter environments like Australia. Nor for blending in there, their white coat having evolved to camouflage them against ice sheets. Their hunting, too, would be different, but primarily as carnivores, their diet could change from consisting primarily of seals to any similar meat.

Two genera of penguin – *Spheniscus* and *Eudyptula* – live in hotter climates (notably, the former as far north as the Galapagos Islands, right on the equator)[120]. However, as this exhibition focuses on anomalies, we can assume that these penguins are of a species not evolved to deal with warmer conditions, and so couldn't survive around the Nile, where average summer temperatures exceed 30 degrees Celsius. The record high for Aswan, where the Nile gives way to the man-made reservoir, Lake Nasser, is 51 degrees Celsius[121]. That's not all, however: the species of penguin we're presuming is represented in the National Museum would lack their primary food supply, the Antarctic krill.

As presented, these are whimsical impossibilities.

But survival of penguins and polar bears in increasingly difficult conditions is a reality as global warming greatly affects their natural environment. While it's believed polar bears take a substantial amount of time to adapt, their hunger means individuals will eat

---

[120] Mueller, Jennifer, 'Where Is The Warmest Climate Penguins Live?'

[121] MacDonald, Jessica, 'Weather In Egypt: Climate, Seasons, And Average Monthly Temperature.'

something other than their current standard food sources. 'A few specialist polar bears might be able to eke out a living on a mixture of seaweed, and fish, and whale carcasses that happen to be around, but eating those kinds of things doesn't sustain anything like the current population levels,' warned Peter Ewins, leader of Arctic conservation for WWF. It's heart-breaking to know that at the time of writing, there are fewer than 25,000 polar bears left in the wild[122]. This ties into the National Museum's implication that polar bears are rare in Australia, even after Total Event Collapse.

We're used to hearing how the planet is heating up, but for penguins living in polar regions, the problem isn't just heat: the number of Antarctic krill has declined by up to 80% since the 1970s. The consequences are demonstrated by the increase of Gentoo penguins, a species with a flexible diet, but rapid decline of the Chinstraps and Adélie species, both massively reliant on these krill. Around 30% of current Adélie penguin colonies may be in decline by 2060, and approximately 60% by 2099[123]. The penguins of the Nile are an anomaly; sadly, penguins in hotter climates are not.

While penguins are anomalously found in Egypt, the Pharaohs of that land have miraculously migrated to the Himalayas. Scantily-clad kings and queens existing in a typically chilly mountain range[124] is a cheerier prospect than the implications for animals –

---

[122] Becker, Rachel A., '4 Ways Polar Bears Are Dealing With Climate Change.'

[123] University of Delaware, 'Penguin Population Could Drop 60 Percent By End Of The Century: Temperature Warming May Have Reached A Tipping Point.'

[124] This is presuming that temperatures are roughly the same as they are now. There's no indication of anything other than the

especially when you consider that, just because the Pharaohs were there, it doesn't necessarily mean their subjects were too. Though, what's a monarch without their kingdom?

The presence of the Daleks is, of course, to fulfil **Doctor Who**'s need to have a physical antagonist in the show. Still, they, and other surrounding exhibits, demonstrate why these anomalies are so troublesome.

'UNIDENTIFIED STONE RELICS

'ROMAN DEITY. PROPHETIC OR EVIDENCE OF "STARS"?'

The 'Roman deity' in question is actually an Auton, found around the Pandorica, alongside the crumbled remains of the Alliance, including complete Daleks and half a Cyberman. Though they're all inert, presumably their proximity to the Pandorica saved their particles, albeit devoid of energy, in a recognisable order. It's only with the light from the Pandorica that a Dalek is partially restored, imbued with potential from the previous universe.

The greatest anomaly, of course, is **all life**. As products of a universe that apparently never happened, this should be obvious, but it gains more credence when considering stars going supernova and how we're made up of their particles. Every atom around us – indeed, every atom that we're comprised of – was once a part of a star that exploded, spreading its components across space-time;

---

status quo – after all, these are labelled anomalies by the museum, so it must be strange for creatures acclimatised to cold environs to live in warm conditions. But we don't know, because the Earth isn't kept alive by our sun but by the exploding TARDIS, seemingly at a different distance from the planet.

even more astonishingly, 'the atoms in your left hand probably came from a different star than did those in your right. We are all, literally, star children, and our bodies made of stardust.'[125]

It's a notion alluded to in similar terms **Doctor Who**, as the Doctor regales Merry Gejelh in *The Rings of Akhaten* (2013):

> 'All the elements in your body were forged many, many millions of years ago, in the heart of a faraway star that exploded and died. That explosion scattered those elements across the desolations of deep space. After so, so many millions of years, these elements came together to form new stars and new planets. And on and on it went. The elements came together and burst apart, forming shoes and ships and sealing wax and cabbages and kings. Until eventually, they came together to make you.'

That covers almost everything you see in *The Big Bang* and more besides – the Doctor's companions; the Stone Dalek; the remnants of aliens; the Underhenge; Aunt Sharon; Amelia's psychiatrist; the National Museum; the printing company responsible for the leaflet advertising 'The Anomaly'; that woman Amelia shoved past in the queue to get closer to the Pandorica; stuffed animals populating the exhibitions; and not forgetting the TARDIS.

Total Event Collapse: the universe literally never happened.

How does the Doctor explain their continued existence? Very simply, that we, and seemingly by extension everything else on Earth (plus our moon), are at the 'eye of the storm, that's all: we're

---

[125] Krauss, Lawrence M, *A Universe From Nothing*, p17.

just the last light to go out.' Meanwhile, the aliens strewn around the Underhenge are 'like after-images. Echoes. Fossils in time. The footprints of the never-were.'[126]

Should the Doctor, then, exist at all? If Gallifrey were erased, the Doctor wouldn't have been born[127]. He could be a footprint too... except that he's a remnant of the universe as it was, trapped inside the Pandorica. Should the Pandorica exist? It was created by alien technology – aliens no longer in existence, fearing for the destruction of a cosmos which never came into being. But if the Pandorica doesn't exist, what stopped the Doctor from averting the TARDIS's destruction? There are no easy answers.

All the core elements of *The Big Bang* are anomalies. This fact is highlighted by the disappearance of Amelia in the Museum, yet the continued existence of Amy.

Narratively, she has done her job, resurrecting Amy and proving a catalyst for the Doctor escaping from the Pandorica. Nonetheless, her unwinding makes older Amy an absolute abnormality

What's the in-universe explanation for this? 'There is no Amelia. From now on, there never was. History is still collapsing,' says the Doctor. 'You're an anomaly. We all are. We're all just hanging on at the eye of the storm. But the eye is closing, and if we don't do something fast, reality will never have happened.'[128] This doesn't

---

[126] *The Big Bang.*

[127] For the purposes of this argument, we will assume that this means their other-universe previous self was never found, as shown in *The Timeless Children* (2020).

[128] *The Big Bang.*

exactly explain why **that version** of the same character remains. We could reason that the Pandorica has something to do with this. We're repeatedly told of the importance of memory, so it's surely no mistake that the remaining Amy is the one who's travelled extensively with the Doctor, and who's most prominent and accurate in his memory. Considering he was trapped in the Pandorica at the point of universal collapse, this could be why she still lives. Knowing that the box has restorative power works into this theory. Equally, the energy conversion required to bring back a Dalek shows how the Pandorica imbues power in whatever its light touches; Amy, having been trapped inside the structure for nearly 2,000 years, would surely have been on the receiving end of this energy too.

With Amy comes a plethora of additional anomalies, hints that the two main people in her life are absent. Amy's engagement ring becomes a focal point for her after her discovery of it in the Doctor's pocket at the end of *The Lodger*. The Doctor encourages her to remember Rory, explaining that 'People fall out of the world sometimes, but they always leave traces. Little things we can't quite account for. Faces in photographs, luggage, half-eaten meals, rings. Nothing is ever forgotten, not completely.' Even at the start of this story, he acknowledges that Amy isn't an ordinary girl. Amy can't cross that barrier just yet, despite the Doctor adding that her house was too big, with too many empty rooms. It's an allusion to Prisoner Zero in *The Eleventh Hour*, but also that her house is an anomaly. 'Does it ever bother you, Amy, that your life doesn't make any sense?'[129] he asks. It soon becomes clear that Amy's life,

---

[129] *The Pandorica Opens.*

throughout the whole of Series 5, is an anomaly. Her backstory – particularly her living with her Aunt Sharon[130] – isn't expanded upon in the previous episodes, though in *The Vampires of Venice*, the Doctor overtly recognises the lack of her father by suggesting he could give her away at Amy and Rory's wedding.

We could credit the TARDIS for the engagement ring's presence: the ship's interior exists in another dimension and operates separately from our fabric of existence, so anomalies could be maintained.

Then there's the photo of Amy in her kissogram outfit and Rory as a Roman centurion at a fancy-dress party, found by the Alliance (and then River) in Amy's room. It forms the basis for the Alliance's creation of Rory as an Auton[131]. Rory was wiped from time in *Cold Blood*, leaving a gap in Amy's life and her reason for joining the Doctor unexplained: after all, she hinted in *The Beast Below* that her travels in the TARDIS were her running away from responsibilities, including her imminent nuptials. Another factor may have filled this void, but that's never expanded upon. It also

---

[130] It's not made clear in *The Eleventh Hour* if Amy's house belongs to Aunt Sharon, although Amelia certainly believed so, as she informs the Doctor that her aunt had moved to England. However, *The Big Bang* shows that it was owned by Tabetha and Augustus Pond, meaning Sharon was living there solely to look after Amelia or lived there with the Ponds anyway, which explains why they own such a sizeable property. Aside from seeing her parents in the house, this is where the crack in time had consumed them.

[131] They're lucky Rory has been erased from time; otherwise, he'd have been travelling in the TARDIS. When turning up to find a duplicate in 102 CE, the Doctor would definitely have considered this a trap.

leaves plot-points unresolved in *The Vampires of Venice* and *Amy's Choice*.

Despite that, these events still happened. Rory never existed, but the Doctor clearly remembers him perfectly well. He accidentally mentions Rory in *Vincent and the Doctor* to Amy, who remains oblivious; he keeps their engagement ring and says it belonged to a friend in *The Pandorica Opens*; and is aware of Amy's subconscious pain, distracting her when Vincent notices she's crying. We can assume, then, that the events of *The Vampires of Venice*, *Amy's Choice*, and *The Hungry Earth / Cold Blood* (2010) all unfolded as we saw, and that Rory was still a part of their collective story. It potentially makes memories themselves anomalous[132].

And so, yes, putting aside the fact Gallifrey would never have existed after Total Event Collapse, the Doctor is furthermore an anomaly in Amy's life and remains so until he's restored at the wedding reception. The Doctor is reduced to being an imaginary friend, the dolls and drawings from Amy's childhood lingering around her room despite the TARDIS never crashing in her garden at Easter 1996. The catalyst for his becoming imaginary is the remnants of the previous universe. 'Well, you'll remember me a bit,' relents the Doctor as Amelia sleeps. 'I'll be a story in your head.'[133]

Fortunately, the Doctor realises that he can hold on through a phrase to revive her memories of the TARDIS... which is curious in

---

[132] Rory's certainly are: his memory is split between his real life in Leadworth and the TARDIS, and his fake Roman life, implanted in him by the Nestene Consciousness.
[133] *The Big Bang*.

itself. The Doctor's link to the TARDIS has long been established[134], but Amy clearly remembers a decent amount about the Doctor already, so why should the TARDIS change things so much? The TARDIS likely symbolises the realisation of her travels in time and space: without it, she and her imaginary friend lacked a means of exploration; with it, knowledge of space-time travel is restored. It's the final piece in the puzzle.

Well, not **quite** the final piece. Fittingly, that's River Song – the person who remains an anomaly longest of all.

She shouldn't exist during this story, except at the very end (which of course leads to her conception anyway) when she cheekily accepts the Doctor's marriage proposal. Her leading the Doctor and Amy to the co-ordinates in the 'Pandorica Opens' painting is an aberration because she can't exist: her own father was erased from time earlier in the series. She also doesn't seem to recognise him, apparently taken aback by seeing Rory on their side after she's rescued from the TARDIS's time loop. True, River lies, and seems quickly to accept the idea of his allegiance. Even so, this leaves a dangling question: can she remember Rory like the Doctor can (because they're both somewhat detached from the conventional timeline) or were those memories erased, as Amy's were[135]?

---

[134] In *The Power of the Daleks* (1966), the Doctor mentions the TARDIS is involved in the process of regeneration, and whenever the TARDIS is in distress, so too is the Doctor.

[135] After Amy questioned why Rory would be wiped from her mind, whereas the Clerics from *Flesh and Stone* weren't, the Doctor replied, 'They weren't part of your world. This is different. This is your own history changing.' (*Cold Blood*)

Either way, her existence relies on Rory and Amy. Similarly, her existence depends on the Doctor, meaning she remains an anomaly when she turns up at her parents' wedding. She's also a product of the TARDIS, and part Time Lord, two things erased as a result of Total Event Collapse. Of course, at this stage, the audience doesn't know River's backstory; still, it makes for an interesting dilemma.

Fortunately, River is used to being an anomaly. She was introduced as such in *Silence in the Library / Forest of the Dead* (2008), unique in 21st-century **Doctor Who** for being a character who meets the Doctor in the wrong order[136]. Her first appearance, from the points of view of the Doctor and the audience, is virtually her last, from her viewpoint (with *The Name of the Doctor* as a coda). And because their chronologies are out of sync, she's a timely abnormality throughout Alex Kingston's time on the show. River turns being anomalous into a trend!

It also repositions River on an even footing with the Doctor. She has somehow survived, while the Doctor hasn't. By giving Amy the diary, River reminds her of what the Doctor told Amelia as a child. She obviously doesn't achieve omniscience, but she at least gives that impression – which becomes an important point when she reminds us that we don't actually know who she is. Her warning in *The Big Bang* to the Doctor, 'You're going to find out very soon now. And I'm sorry, but that's when everything changes', is as much a warning to us, and recalls her mention of the Pandorica

---

[136] Though Mel Bush's introduction in 'Terror of the Vervoids' (*The Trial of a Time Lord* episodes 9 to 12) is out of order, and never expanded upon on-screen, the rest of her adventures play out in a linear fashion.

opening at the conclusion of *Flesh and Stone*. By being independent of him and the TARDIS (unlike the Ponds who, until *The God Complex*, spend the majority of their time travelling with him), River maintains a life away from his sphere of influence.

Their status quo is established immediately in her first appearance in Series 4, where she holds all the cards. She's the one who lures the Doctor to the Library using the psychic paper, calls out his bad behaviour, and knows what happens to Donna Noble. She knows his future self and refuses to share any of that knowledge; she stops him peeking at her diary and claims it's by his own decree. The Doctor figures out the problem, but River makes the heroic sacrifice – in a selfish way, not wanting their future together erased (and of course, because her existence relies on his meeting Amy). But she doesn't seem to do it for 'timey-wimey' reasons: the sacrifice comes from the heart.

Their one-upmanship reaches two conclusions: in *The Name of the Doctor* (where she asks, 'I was mentally linked with Clara; if she's really dead, then how can I still be here?', knowing Clara survives her trip through the Doctor's timeline and perhaps had greater significance in his life) and *The Husbands of River Song*, in which the pair end up on Darillium, where River is destined to spend her final night. It's only in the closing minute of the episode that the 12th Doctor reveals that last trick up his sleeve: a night on Darillium lasts 24 years.

So how does River exist as an anomaly for so long? Potentially, it's because she's a complicated space-time event whose life is entwined so intricately with the Doctor's, and who takes a crucial role in the fixed point at Lake Silencio, that time makes a concession for her. It's a romantic notion – that some people are too important to be simply forgotten and that a life is measured by its impact on others – and that, too, is at the core of Steven Moffat's storytelling.

Secondly, we can't forget River's time spent in a time loop, protected by the TARDIS. Let's posit that the TARDIS works similarly to the Pandorica: cut off from the rest of space-time, potentially from the multiverse, it would contain particles from the previous iteration of the universe and contains 'a moment of infinite power'[137]. This energy could, theoretically, maintain River too, akin to how it's cultivated life on Earth.

Considering the TARDIS transmits to 'every particle of space and time simultaneously'[138], it might even paradoxically explain River's presence outside the TARDIS's continuum at points when she shouldn't still exist[139].

However, the TARDIS cannot easily be explained either. As technology from a planet that 'never happened' in Total Event Collapse, it can't be on Earth. It can't have been grown. And it can't have exploded either. In a universe undone by the explosion of the TARDIS, the explosion could never have occurred.

The TARDIS would eventually be extinguished alongside the rest of the cosmos, but the paradoxical nature of this problem is especially interesting. The implication is an exaggeration of a theory on how

---

[137] *The Big Bang.*
[138] *The Big Bang.*
[139] We'll come back to these points because they may tell us more than upon initial examination.

space-time operates, specifically how we explain conditions in the very earliest instances of the universe, which we can't currently comprehend. That complication is how the cosmos could have existed as a supremely focused ball of potential. How can the energy now spreading – right this very second as you read this – further and further out into nothingness, have been contained in such a small singularity as the Big Bang suggests? 'We do not have any theory that describes the universe at ultra-high temperatures and ultra-high densities,' said Anna Ijjas of the Max Planck Institute for Gravitational Physics. To combat this, another notion has been put forward: that our universe has emerged from another[140]. After its intense contraction, reality was confined and expanded once more. Under this notion, matter still existed in a hugely refined form, the radius of just 10^{-25} centimetres, 'more than a billion times smaller than the radius of an electron.' Its size remains mind-boggling but feels more reasonable than explaining how everything we experience and far more besides came out of inexplicable nothingness[141].

The Big Bang doesn't take things to this endpoint. The universe doesn't end – not quite. Just before it does so, Earth sits in the middle of a tornado and from the last whimpers of our universe, the Doctor, with help from Amy, reboots existence. What would have occurred after the complete reduction of space-time is never explored, but the anomalies are vital.

Another theory posits that the Big Bang wasn't the beginning of

---

[140] See Chapter 6.
[141] Amit, Gilead, 'How Did Reality Get Started?' *New Scientist* Vol. 245 #3267.

everything, but instead, everything in its prevailing form. This could be explained by superpositioning[142], and the concept of a 'participatory universe', i.e. determined by consciousness, in which our own perceptions of the cosmos shape reality[143]. Think of it as comparing solid, liquid, and gas. Matter existing outside its current form is an elusive concept, so imagine this universe as a gas and the previous as a liquid. The Big Bang is the process of condensation, a heating up of particles to transform them into another composition. The core ingredients remain, but the properties are different.

Sometimes, under scrutiny, plots unwind and threads come loose – not so in **Doctor Who** Series 5. There are enough established 'timey-wimey' rules and exposition to make the story's conclusion work. The key is the Doctor's description of us as 'the last light going out'[144]. This might tie into the notion of 'The Big Crunch', the constriction of matter back to its origin point. Instead of its contraction back to the centre of the universe, space-time could fold back to Earth, where the collapse began. With the Pandorica and the TARDIS both here, it makes sense for the reality to be maintained longer than in the rest of the universe. Essentially, the far reaches of the cosmos are affected first, then a domino effect takes the rest of reality, leaving us as the final piece to fall. Alternatively, think of the Earth as a plague carrier. Everyone reacts to an illness differently, so an infected individual could pass on the disease to many others before succumbing to it themself.

---

[142] See Chapter 6.

[143] Brooks, Michael, 'Here. There. Everywhere?' *New Scientist* Vol. 246 #3280.

[144] *The Big Bang*.

The Doctor doesn't kickstart a new universe, per se; he uses the dregs of the universe to bring back order and chaos as we recognise it. Matter isn't reduced to nothing then transformed into a new state. It's reconstituted.

Without these various anomalies, that wouldn't have been possible at all.

CHAPTER 4: WHEN TIME TRAVEL WOULDN'T HELP

RORY

But you're not in the Pandorica.

THE DOCTOR

Yes, I am. Well, I'm not now, but I was back then. Well, back **now** from your point of view, which is back **then** from my point of view. Time travel – you can't keep it straight in your head.[145]

In his review of *The Big Bang* in *Doctor Who Magazine*[146], Graham Kibble-White made a good point: it's difficult to think of a story in which the Doctor travelling back in time to help himself out of a tricky situation wouldn't solve all the problems. He does this to free himself from the Pandorica, revive Amy, and save the sonic screwdriver from presumably being lost in 102 CE. He does it to give himself more time to link the vortex manipulator to the Pandorica. And he does it to save himself from unravelling completely, planting the idea of Amelia's imaginary friend in her head.

So why doesn't the Doctor do this more often? Why does it feel justified in Series 5? And why wouldn't it work, either emotionally or narratively, elsewhere?

The central means of time travel in **Doctor Who** is, obviously, the

---

[145] *The Big Bang.*
[146] DWM #424.

TARDIS. In the early days, a major driving force in narratives was the team's inability to get back to the ship[147]. They've been similarly cut off from it several times in the intervening years – whether due to its seeming destruction[148], through system failure[149], forcibly by others[150], or through the Doctor's death[151]. But anyone arguing that this stops the Doctor changing time is ignoring the fact that they **do** get back to it at the end of each tale (with a few exceptions), so could potentially use it to travel backwards in time to solve problems previously faced.

The general consensus is that the Doctor is an amateur when it comes to the TARDIS, but that's not entirely fair. If they're so poor at piloting, how come they spend so much time on the Doctor's favourite planet? Up to the end of the 12th Doctor's tenure, around 47% of stories take place on Earth, 33% on alien worlds, 16% on spacecraft, and 4% in other realms[152]. In 21st-century **Doctor Who**, the Doctor typically has more luck landing on contemporary Earth, though in reality that is due to the series structure established by Davies, in which the companions' familial lives play an important part in the show[153].

---

[147] For example, in *Marco Polo*, *The Keys of Marinus*, and *The Sensorites* (all 1964).
[148] *The Mind Robber* (1968); *Frontios* (1984).
[149] *Rise of the Cybermen / The Age of Steel* (2006); *Flatline* (2014).
[150] *The War Games*; *Genesis of the Daleks* (1975).
[151] *Father's Day* (2005); *Turn Left* (2008).
[152] Scott, Cavan, and Mark Wright, *Who-Ology: The Official Miscellany*, p227.
[153] The obvious exception is *Aliens of London* (2005), which changes the definition of 'contemporary Earth' throughout Davies'

Some situations play havoc with the TARDIS, so limit the Doctor's ability to change events – despite the Doctor's insistence that their people created black holes, they do interfere with the ship. In *The Impossible Planet*, the TARDIS doesn't want to land on Krop Tor, while *World Enough and Time / The Doctor Falls* (2017) establishes that capsules can't be used on short hops in the vicinity of a black hole[154]. Elsewhere, the Master flew his TARDIS too close and burnt out his dematerialisation circuit[155].

Let's not forget that the TARDIS was presumably awaiting repairs when the Doctor stole her. The TARDIS factored this in by including a substantial Fault Locator, notably used in *The Daleks* (1963-64) then *The Edge of Destruction* (1964), 'the largest piece of machinery in the control room at the time – a great computer bank taking up an entire wall, constantly analysing the TARDIS systems and detecting defects in individual components.'[156] While subsequent control rooms had this feature, they didn't give it prominence; nonetheless, we may assume potential malfunctions would stop the Doctor altering the past.

Unusually, it's not the TARDIS that allows the Doctor to travel back in time in *The Big Bang*; it's a vortex manipulator, acquired by River from Dorium Maldovar, 'fresh off the wrist of a handsome Time Agent'[157], possibly Captain Jack Harkness, who wears one during his

---

stewardship as the Doctor takes Rose back a year late; every subsequent tale set in the present day is actually set 12 months ahead of airdates, until Steven Moffat takes charge.

[154] *World Enough and Time*.
[155] *The Doctor Falls*.
[156] Tribe, Steve, *Doctor Who: The TARDIS Handbook*, p47.
[157] *The Pandorica Opens*.

time with the ninth and 10th Doctors. It's an inaccurate device when we see it then, although Jack must have some proficiency to avoid 'volcano day' during his scams[158]. Otherwise, he uses it as a scanner and projector.

It appears using the vortex manipulator to travel in time is more difficult than using its other functions. Captain Jack uses it after *The Parting of the Ways* to get to 1869 before the device burns out, stranding him in the 19th century, but we don't witness it first-hand. In Series 3, the Family of Blood used a stolen one to track the Doctor and Martha, but we don't see that either. This means the first time we actually **see** the manipulator used to travel in time is in *The Sound of Drums*, enhanced by the Doctor to get himself, Martha, and Jack to 2008 after being stranded on Malcassairo.

The manipulator's reliability understandably varies marginally depending on user: River is most confident with it, alongside Missy. While the former considers it 'a bike through traffic'[159], Missy agrees with the 11th and 13th Doctors that it's 'cheap and nasty time travel'[160], alluding to a fair degree of imprecision[161].

Nonetheless, River is so adept with it, it's likely the Doctor can use it fairly accurately too. They could surely rely on a vortex manipulator if they wanted to tweak timelines.

Why don't they? There are two core reasons – the first of which we

---

[158] *The Empty Child / The Doctor Dances.*
[159] *The Angels Take Manhattan* (2012).
[160] Respectively, *The Magician's Apprentice* (2015), *The Big Bang*, and *Spyfall* Part 2 (2020).
[161] Clara has a 100% success rate, however.

can infer from the unusual conditions the Doctor finds himself in during the Series 5 finale.

In *The Big Bang*, as the universe collapses around them, the Doctor explains to Rory that using the manipulator is a 'rubbish way to time travel, but the universe is tiny now. We'll be fine.' Think of space-time like a thriving mass of paths, cul-de-sacs, T-junctions, and roundabouts. It's a thoroughfare stretched across 10 dimensions[162]. Total Event Collapse has tarmacked over everything and cleared the road. Gone, too, are the signposts because you don't need them. There's a long, winding boulevard and even that's eroding.

Still, the TARDIS remains the most impressive ship in sci-fi, so it's churlish to think it can't achieve in normal circumstances what the Vortex Manipulator does under unusual ones. In fact, in *A Christmas Carol* (2010), it does: the TARDIS zips back and forth across Kazran Sardick's life, and takes him, the Doctor, and Abigail on trips across time and space – then returns them to staggered Christmas Days.

The precedent is set by Steven Moffat's first **Doctor Who** work, the short story 'Continuity Errors', in the anthology *Decalog 3: Consequences* (1996). This features the seventh Doctor attempting to check out a restricted book from the Library of New Alexandria, only to be met with a frosty librarian who simply won't let him. The Doctor tries to rewrite the librarian's life so she's more forthcoming, but a happier existence by his hand doesn't mean she'll relinquish the text. The Time Lord even goes as far as calling

---

[162] According to superstring theory.

himself a doctor of history, and, when questioned if he means he studies it, he retorts, 'I mean I make it better.' It's the similar laissez-faire attitude to time travel displayed by the Master in Moffat's other 20th-century **Doctor Who** work, *The Curse of Fatal Death* (1999). In this charity skit, the Doctor's arch-nemesis repeatedly travels back in time to lay traps for the Doctor.

It's fair to say that Steven Moffat's **Doctor Who** used time travel as a core element more than any other era of the programme. While 20th-century **Doctor Who** seldom explored the consequences of tampering with the fourth dimension, even the stories Moffat wrote for the show before becoming showrunner largely used time travel to drive the narrative: *The Girl in the Fireplace* focused on the life of Madame de Pompadour, splintered across time frames in a spaceship; the Weeping Angels absorb potential energy left by time displacements in *Blink* (2007); the fifth and 10th Doctors meet in *Time Crash* (2007) and the latter saves the TARDIS from destruction because the former had already seen him do it; and the 10th Doctor and River Song meet out of sequence in *Silence in the Library / Forest of the Dead*.

But while Moffat doesn't typically abide by the programme's rules, the Doctor surely does. This is the second main reason the Doctor doesn't meddle with time too frequently: there **are** rules. Even when they consider themself the last of their species, these rules are so ingrained that they rarely stretch them[163]. As much is

---

[163] In *Spyfall*, the 13th Doctor does something similar to what the 11th does in *The Big Bang*: she goes back in time to plant a series of instructions in the aeroplane to save her companions. This shows that guidelines can at least be bent, if there's enough

evident from the TARDIS.

The TARDIS is a product of Time Lord technology, so it's reasonable to assume that certain laws against interference are programmed into it. She doesn't like the Doctor trying to rewrite time in *Before the Flood*, refusing to take him back further than when he materialised. Though the Doctor flaunts the strictures of his own people, by and large there are some things they refuse to do. 'Some things are fixed; some things are in flux. Pompeii is fixed,' he elaborates in *The Fires of Pompeii*. 'Because that's how I see the universe. Every waking second, I can see what is, what was, what could be, what must not. That's the burden of a Time Lord, Donna.'

We glimpse this mentality, albeit in a comical fashion, in another 10th Doctor tale. In *Smith and Jones* (2007), the Doctor actively chooses not to do anything that will affect the eventual outcome. He travels back to before Martha gets into work and removes his tie as a reminder to Martha later in the day that she'd already met him before he met her. 'But hold on,' Martha realises. 'If you could see me this morning, why didn't you tell me not to go in to work?'

'Crossing into established events is strictly forbidden,' the Doctor warns. 'Except for cheap tricks.'

That's vital. No matter how good a pilot (or negotiator, as the 12th Doctor would have it) each incarnation is, the Doctor isn't supposed to interfere; more than that, they certainly aren't allowed to cross their own timeline. The 10th Doctor implies as much in *The Girl in the Fireplace*. It's specifically established the Doctor **can't** rewrite events using the TARDIS.

---

incentive.

It's a point similarly raised by Rose in *The Parting of the Ways* (2005). She asks why they can't go back a week or so to warn the inhabitants of the Game Station about the Daleks; it'd also give the Doctor time to build the Delta Wave. The ninth Doctor replies, 'As soon as the TARDIS lands in that second, I become part of events, stuck in the timeline.'

We occasionally see the complications of time travel (and so can relate to the rule of non-interference), specifically how small errors or selfishness can lead to paradoxes. Stories like *The Space Museum* (1965), *The Claws of Axos* (1971), *Day of the Daleks* (1972), *The Armageddon Factor*, *Meglos* (1980), *Mawdryn Undead* (1983), and *The Lodger* demonstrate how dangerous it is to mess with time. It's something that irks the fourth Doctor in *Image of the Fendahl* (1977), branding the Time Lords 'criminal' for putting Planet 5 in a time loop. The 11th Doctor suffers for his dalliances with paradoxes, his timelines unravelling with only Amy capable of saving him; it's a consequence he's prepared for, but can't have been a pleasant experience.

Of course, there's one simple truth of time travel in science fiction: all too often, the rules only apply when they're convenient to the plot. The Doctor's mastery of the fourth dimension changes according entirely to what suits the narrative best.

Steven Moffat pointed out that the hero of **Doctor Who** experiences the universe in the wrong order, so, when reality collapses, the gloves are off: 'The rules are out – he is going to cheat to stop this. He's not sticking to the rulebook this week. He's got a very small amount of time to stop all of reality never happening in the first place.'[164]

This Get Out Of Jail Free card feels justified. It's what the Doctor would do when he's got absolutely no choice. And he hasn't. All of time and space never existed! There's no other solution. The vortex manipulator's usage is established, and only serves to save the Doctor from the Pandorica. It isn't used to reboot the universe (apart from transporting the Doctor to where he needs to be). It makes emotional sense as well, surely the major driving force in all great narratives. As long as you believe in and care about these characters, you'll let writers get away with an awful lot.

Fittingly, the real reason we give *The Big Bang* a free pass is a paradox. It works because it works. Sometimes, it's best not to question the magic.

---

[164] *Out of Time.*

CHAPTER 5: THE TROUBLE WITH TIME

'The universe is big. It's vast and complicated and ridiculous,
and sometimes – very rarely – impossible things just
happen, and we call them miracles. And that's the theory.
900 years; never seen one yet, but this would do me.'

[The Doctor][165]

You're wandering around, talking to someone you love. They
become your entire focus. You're not worried about your phone or
your Fitbit or looming deadlines at work. Time is immaterial here.
Nonetheless, the inevitable happens. You look down at your watch.
A few hours have passed, impossibly. How did that even happen?

We mark time by our own body cycles – the need to eat at certain
points in a day, or the urge to sleep – on small, daily scales. On
universal scales, time fizzles to nothing, beyond our frame of
reference. Time's funny like that: it's dictated by lots of massive
things, but means something different to each of us. Because the
first really important thing you need to know is that time is a
personal thing. It's up to you how you spend it.

Time is complicated. Even aside from anomalies, time behaves
rather strangely in *The Pandorica Opens / The Big Bang*.

So let's begin at the end, shall we?

---

[165] *The Pandorica Opens.*

The Doctor's Timestream Unravels

'I escaped then. Brilliant. I love it when I do that.'

[The Doctor][166]

After the Pandorica flies into the heart of the exploding TARDIS, the universe is restored. But the Doctor is trapped outside. His timestream begins unravelling and he experiences recent events backwards.

Every **Doctor Who** tale shatters 'time's arrow'[167]. This isn't a description of what time actually is, but instead how we feel its flow. Time's arrow is a simple concept, and one we're all experiencing right now. Your existence goes in a set order, as does the world around you. The direction of time's arrow separates life from death. What's done is done.

If that's a grim proposition, remember, too, that it's resulted in everything around you. You've learnt how to speak and read and forgotten neither; a butterfly can't revert to its caterpillar state; the popcorn you're eating won't go back to being raw corn.

Time's arrow dictates that we constantly move forwards. **Doctor Who** plays with that idea as it revolves around time travel. For each individual person, their chronology moves forward; the same can be said for the people they talk to and the places the TARDIS lands in. However, the TARDIS effectively bends the space-time continuum by pushing itself backwards and forwards in time.

---

[166] *The Big Bang.*

[167] A term popularised by Sir Arthur Eddington in his 1928 book *The Nature of the Physical World.*

Essentially, life goes on as normal for the individuals, but the presence of the Doctor, their companions, and their ship is only possible through the arrow's bending.

When we talk about time, what we're actually talking about is two things: personal perception (encompassing light and gravity) and heat. The latter is harder to account for because, though we see its consequences, it's easier to relate such an intangible concept through connections to self. For instance, we see a glass fall and shatter, and panic about all those shards spread across the floor; the only time we consider is the amount we'll use cleaning it up. We generally don't think about how time was involved in its undoing (though we may curse gravity).

Time is too ephemeral a concept for us to accurately understand. Similarly, the universe is so vast that, if we properly appreciated its immensity, we'd get nothing else done. It's astounding to consider that our heads are travelling faster through time than our feet. Tell your mates to astonish them, but don't go into the nitty-gritty. What this equates to on an everyday basis is practically nothing. In a lifetime, it's negligible. A one-foot difference amounts to 90 billionths of a second over a lifetime measured at 79 years[168]. While it's true that your head will always be older than your toes – and someone living in mountain ranges ages faster than someone at or below sea level – this won't make any difference to your life whatsoever.

Travel a little upwards and you begin to appreciate the conflicting

---

[168] Boyle, Rebecca, 'In Test of Relativity Theory, Superaccurate Atomic Clocks Prove Your Head Ages Nanoseconds Faster than Your Feet.'

forces of the cosmos. The International Space Station and its full crew of six are constantly falling towards Earth, yet they remain an average 240 miles (400km) from the planet's surface. This is because it's also travelling horizontally at around 17,150 miles (27600.25km) an hour[169]. Not all things are equal, however: these astronauts:

> 'age a little less because of the velocity at which they travel, and a little more for enjoying less of the gravity of Earth. The effects do not quite cancel out. Velocity wins, leaving each ISS astronaut who completes a six-month tour of duty 0.007 seconds younger than someone who stayed on Earth.'[170]

What's imperceptibly tiny to us has grander consequences for the universe. Gravity affects time; we know this from Einstein, who transformed our thinking of the fabric of reality by positing the idea of space-time as a connected form. The greater a mass, the more its gravitational pull and the greater its effects on time. Stretch some clingfilm out. That's space-time. Now drop a ball onto it; the clingfilm will sag downwards. That's how an object warps the fabric of reality. You can place smaller and larger objects across the film and their effects will differ. That brings us to what we really know about time, the first thing being that it's relative. Time isn't an absolute. It differs all across the universe. The closer you are to a gravitational field's source, the slower time will move.

Admittedly, none of this exactly explains how the Doctor's personal timeline can unravel, nor how time can go backwards. To get to the

---

[169] Battersby, Stephen, ed, *Where The Universe Came From*, p8.
[170] Battersby, *Where The Universe Came From*, p34.

bottom of those mysteries, we have to go back further. Our relationship with time is at the heart of Series 5.

Temporal Loops

'I'm sorry, my love.'

[River Song][171]

The TARDIS explodes. Again and again. Throughout time, it explodes. But what happens to anything or anyone inside? River Song is trapped in a temporal loop, reliving the ship's destruction, and effectively, her own death. It's a nasty way to go, but of course, the TARDIS does this to save her. As a child of the TARDIS, you can understand its desire to save her.

The loop seemingly lasts 15 seconds[172], and if we gather it's been exploding since 102 CE, River died 'approximately 3,981,945,600 times before the Doctor saves her'[173]. Even that's questionable, though, because we don't know when the TARDIS **did** blow up. It can't have done so on the day the TARDIS lands at the end of *The Pandorica Opens*: that's 23 June 2010 and it does take off again. It can't have been 1,894 years before that either, because without it acting as a star, life wouldn't have crawled out of the primordial soup. The Doctor says it's exploding at every point in history, so time might be immaterial here. It has happened, is happening, and will happen, all at once. The loop is simultaneously infinite, 15 seconds, and no time at all.

---

[171] *The Pandorica Opens / The Big Bang.*
[172] Or that's what we see. The audience experiences an edited version, so the sequence must've continued longer than that.
[173] Maddox, Twitter, February 2020.

Once more, it's a matter of perspective. We can only hope River didn't live through that infinity, or at least can't remember it. This presumes that the energy required to replay the situation affects the memory of the looped, meaning River's destined to do the same actions again without displaying new initiatives. She has no free will when the outcome is predetermined. Nevertheless, she at least recognises that she's been caught in the loop, quipping, 'And what sort of time do you call this?' when the Doctor eventually saves her.

The big problem of time is knowing **what it is**. Go on: try to describe it. You'll say that June gives way to July or that 1pm comes after 12 noon. You might throw the phrase 'cause and effect' in there for good measure. We know how it can drag in boring meetings. We recognise when something's over with too quickly. And there's never enough of it, is there? Our idea of time is, understandably, human-centric.

Our perception of time is so vital to our thinking that we can't consider an existence without it. Cause and effect are so integrated in our minds that separating or reversing them is an overwhelming task. It's not simply reading a sentence backwards.

When learning about cause and effect, they're shown through demonstrative scenarios, like that previously mentioned glass dropping on the floor. However, they boil down to the minuscule too: you're reading this sentence. Now this one. And now this. You might check this footnote[174]. Moving back and reading the quote at the start of this chapter, or indeed any previous pages, involves the

---

[174] 'As my will, so mote it be!' (The Master, *The Dæmons*.)

forward movement of time.

If someone plays a video or song backwards, you recognise that because our sense of time is intrinsic to our consciousness. Even if the reversal is subtle, you'll probably feel uneasy and realise something's wrong.

Language psychologist Chris Sinha suggests that 'space and time seem to be closely related domains of human cognition [...] We speak of events occurring in relation to temporal landmarks, the same way that we locate objects in relation to spatial landmarks.'[175] In *The Runaway Bride* (2006), the 10th Doctor describes it thus: 'The human race makes sense out of chaos. Marking it out with weddings and Christmas and calendars.'

Take, for instance, our reliance on the latter. **The Simpsons** (1989-) neatly jokes about how we measure time in *Treehouse of Horror VI* (1995) as Homer complains of 'lousy Smarch weather', Springfield Elementary School having misprinted its calendars to include a 13th 28-day month. And in *Mountain of Madness* (1997), Bart checks his watch and asks Lisa what comes after 12. When she tells him, he corrects her, 'No, **after** 12.' BJ Novak, star of **The Office** (2005-13), similarly poked fun when suggesting a calendar comprised of 1,000 days a year, divided into 25 months, with 40 days a month. He amended this so that months would be 30 days instead of 40, because people hate January. When trying to explain that January is merely a label, that ending January would make no difference, he was ignored. Novak further argues that 'I want to double the length

---

[175] Sinha, Chris, 'A Life Without Time.' *New Scientist* #2833, October 2011.

93

of a second so people won't always have to say, "Can you give me two seconds?" They can just say, "One second." I have a lot of ideas like that.'[176]

Birthdays, Christmas, anniversaries, April Fool's Day, Valentine's Day, New Year's: marking out our lives in such ways could seem ridiculous when you step back from it, but it's not just a joking matter. It's become an obsession: for most of human history, we've gathered the time of day by looking to the sky and estimating, based on the position of the sun. Rough calculations in our minds resulted in sun dials, but now, we take 'atomically precise cues from our phones and computers not once or twice a day, but continuously and compulsively.'[177]

In 2015, there was a case of 'chronic déjà vu', in which a 23-year-old claimed he was experiencing time loops. He would have a sense of déjà vu – French for 'already seen', wherein an individual feels a sense of familiarity with a person, place, conversation, or event as if the same thing had happened before – then further 'déjà vu of the déjà vu'. Psychologist Dr Akira O'Connor considered déjà vu as 'a sort of "brain twitch". Just as we get muscle spasms, or eye twitches, it could be that the bit of your brain which sends signals to do with familiarity and memory is firing out of turn.'[178]

If time is relative to matter, it's also relative to observers. Think about when you're on a moving bus and see a plane in the sky. For a short period, it looks still, suspended in the sky, defying time and

---

[176] Novak, BJ, 'The Man Who Invented The Calendar.'
[177] Garfield, Simon, *Timekeepers*, p4.
[178] Ailes, Emma, 'Terrifying Time Loop: The Man Trapped In Constant Déjà Vu.'

gravity. Fortunately, time soon catches up with the plane and it carries on its travels. For you, it stopped; for the people inside the plane, it continued as normal. But imagine you can spontaneously relocate onto the plane. You're now experiencing things at the same pace as the people on the plane.

Apply this principle to the wider universe. Our view of time is partially defined by light, a major factor in everything we perceive. Look at the night sky and you'll see an immense gallery of stars; the light that reaches your eyes, however, has travelled an incredibly long distance. Limited by the speed of light, you're essentially looking into the past. Those stars live and die in their own timeframes, and we're seeing part of their existence.

That's what happens for the Doctor when he transmats into the exploding TARDIS to rescue River. He interrupts the recognised timeline (we may infer that the TARDIS does some heavy lifting to accommodate that) and so switches his viewpoint. The audience sees him appear once; for all we know, he's done that ad infinitum as a new chronology is established – then interrupts it again when teleporting himself and River out. Now, they can run off with Amy and Rory to reboot the universe, while the TARDIS carries on its perpetual decline.

The Fabric of Space-Time

'Today, just dying is a result.'

[The Doctor][179]

The time loop in the TARDIS shows an isolated space-time, where

---

[179] *The Big Bang*.

matter exists separately from the rest of the universe. It can be interrupted, as the Doctor does, but typically, it runs at its own pace and in its own place. The same is true of the Pandorica. That's how Amy survives. Aside from being shot, she should have aged across the 1,894 years or, a grimmer proposition, decayed – but the Pandorica forces its occupant to stay alive, because, as the 'perfect prison', it contains, 'perfectly preserved, a few billion atoms of the universe as it was.'[180]

It's easy to note that space-time exists as a somewhat intangible form of reality, but that implies that space and time are symbiotic and cannot exist without each other. Yet our experiences tell us differently. We can move freely in space, but our position in time feels fixed. This is on the understanding that, of the four dimensions we definitely experience[181], three are space, and the fourth is time. Space consists of length, width, and height, so moving forwards in a straight line is one dimension; turning left or right entails a second; and jumping at the same time requires the third. The fourth dimension, time, separates those actions.

Thank the fourth dimension that life makes sense.

This is best described by the 12th Doctor in *The Pilot*:

> 'Time doesn't pass. The passage of time is an illusion, and life is the magician. Because life only lets you see one day at a time. You remember being alive yesterday; you hope

---

[180] *The Big Bang.*

[181] Superstring theory postulates that there are 10 dimensions; however, as the further six account for alternate planes, it remains theoretical – as do the 11 dimensions of M-Theory.

96

you're going to be alive tomorrow; so it feels like you're travelling from one to the other. But nobody's moving anywhere. Movies don't really move. They're just pictures – lots and lots of pictures. All of them still; none of them moving. Just frozen moments. But if you experience those pictures one after the other, then everything comes alive...

'Imagine if time all happened at once. Every moment of your life laid out around you like a city. Streets full of buildings made of days. The day you were born; the day you die. The day you fall in love; the day that love ends. A whole city built from triumph and heartbreak and boredom and laughter and cutting your toenails. It's the best place you will ever be.

'Time is a structure relative to ourselves. Time is the space made by our lives where we stand together, forever.

'Time And Relative Dimension In Space. It means life.'

Accounting for the Doctor's proposition, whereas we experience events as cause to effect, in a place where 'all possible configurations of matter exist... there is no passage of time, merely a set of unconnected instants... [T]he comforting illusion of time should be infinite too. If time doesn't exist, it won't end.'[182]

We'll come back to the idea of the universe's expansion, but for now, let's surmise that the energy that pushes matter outwards from the Big Bang creates new space. We tend to think of space as an ever-extending sheet – which begs the question, what is space

---

[182] Battersby, Stephen, 'The End Of Time'. *New Scientist* #2833.

expanding **into**? Universal expansion theorises that space-time is everything, so doesn't expand 'into' anything; instead, the gaps between space are getting larger as galaxies, for example, drift apart. Don't think of space as expanding in a container, occupying more of the container and thus replacing whatever was there before; 'we envision space stretching, and in the process creating new space that the universe and its contents can then occupy. Space expands, and hence grows, by virtue of creating new space.'[183]

Professor Richard Miller theorises that new packets of time are created as the universe expands too: 'It suddenly occurred to me that the flow of time was really a gradual addition of new moments in time, new "nows".'[184] This may account for pockets of time existing within another sector of space-time, just as they seem to inside the TARDIS (itself in its own dimension anyway) and inside the Pandorica. The box boasts security features like 'deadlocks, time stops, matter lines'[185] – it's all technobabble, except that the Doctor's insistence that 'it forces you to stay alive'[186] by stasis-locking the occupant implies that the Pandorica exists in its own pocket of space-time. This then acts as a seal, stopping anyone inside from dying and any particles from escaping once locked. This pocket of localised time can clearly influence, and be influenced by, what goes on around it: how else could it revive Amy through a

---

[183] Greene, Brian, 'Ask Brian Greene: What Exactly Is The Universe Expanding Into?'
[184] Matthews, Robert, 'Where Does Time Come From?' *Science Focus*, May 2017.
[185] *The Pandorica Opens*.
[186] *The Big Bang*.

sample of living DNA or bring the Dalek back through its restoration field?

Which aliens in the Alliance could create such a prison? The Daleks are the likeliest candidate, seeing as they were shown to have mastered time travel[187] and fought in the Time War. The Sontarans were forbidden to interfere in that war[188], although they had some time-travel capabilities[189]. The Cybermen have knowledge of the multiverse and also have time-travel capability[190], and the Zygons, in *The Day of the Doctor*, demonstrate a willingness to utilise 'timey-wimey' technology. You'd think the Judoon, working for the Shadow Proclamation, would have some grasp of time travel, but it belies the 10th Doctor's claim that they're 'completely thick'[191]. They don't grasp the implications of anomalies, instead insisting on 'two fugitives, two payments' in *Fugitive of the Judoon* (2020) when the 13th Doctor reveals she's **also** the Time Lord they've been paid to track down – in addition to the Doctor they've already captured.

Mind you, there are at least 10,000 ships circling the planet so we see a **very** small sample of them in the Underhenge. If the Daleks were capable of putting together the Pandorica entirely by

---

[187] Certainly in *The Chase* but it's implied in *The Dalek Invasion of Earth* (1964) too.

[188] *The Sontaran Stratagem* (2008).

[189] *The Time Warrior* (1973-74) shows they have primitive time-travel technology.

[190] They have a captured timeship in *Attack of the Cybermen* (1985), and the Cybermen first seen in *The Haunting of Villa Diodati* (2020) definitely can travel through time, even before the Master's upgrades in *The Timeless Children*.

[191] *Smith and Jones*.

themselves, they wouldn't have searched for help. It's fair to call this plan a joint effort.

Either way, we see another example of pockets of time and how matter from one can interact with another as the Doctor is forced to rewind his life. *The Big Bang* shows a correlation between space and time that's at one instant adhered to and the next argued against. We can justify both approaches using the old adage that time is relative. From the Doctor's point of view, after he reboots the universe, time goes backwards. But not entirely: the events he witnesses aren't happening backwards, so when he talks to Amy in the *Byzantium*, neither speaks backwards. Their actions are very much forwards too. Essentially, they exist in a pocket of time, though the Doctor experiences these pockets in a reversed fashion.

Time isn't relative entirely to a person; it has a wider sphere, affected by larger contexts. Consider the instructions on seed packets, with directions for when and where to sow them. Although gardeners can ignore these, planting them in accordance with seasonal guidelines will get the best outcome. That's what happens to the Doctor: he briefly gets embroiled in instances of time, and experiences those in a linear fashion before his personal timeline reverts to a bending of time's arrow.

The space-time relationship is reinforced: as space contracts, so too does time. While this unravelling increases, they seem to happen concurrently. Still, Amelia disappears before Amy, so perhaps as her frame of reference is 1996 whereas Amy's is at the point of Total Event Collapse, 102 CE. Her sphere of influence is more complicated than that, of course: she was born in 1989, met the Doctor in April 1996, obsessed over him until he returned in

2008, then left in the TARDIS in 2010. Her continued existence after Amelia's erasure is a total paradox.

Where Do You Get Your Ideas From?

'Okay, kid – this is where it gets complicated.'

[Amy][192]

It's the question that plagues fiction writers. 'You get ideas from daydreaming. You get ideas from being bored. You get ideas all the time', wrote Neil Gaiman. 'The only difference between writers and other people is we notice when we're doing it. You get ideas when you ask yourself simple questions. The most important of the questions is just, "What if...?"'[193]

The other response can be found in **Sherlock** (2010-): 'The wheel turns. Nothing is ever new.'[194]

That's where *The Big Bang* comes in. Where exactly did the Doctor get the idea to escape the Pandorica? When did that thought occur to him? What about his idea to reboot the universe?

Five years before *Under the Lake / Before the Flood* explained the concept to viewers, *The Big Bang* featured the Bootstrap Paradox too. The term originates from the Robert A Heinlein novella, *By His Bootstraps*, published in the October 1941 edition of *Astounding Science Fiction*, which explores a paradox as a result of time travel. It's otherwise known as a causal loop, predestination paradox, or ontological paradox, and can be defined as a self-originating

---

[192] *The Big Bang.*
[193] Gaiman, Neil, 'Where Do You Get Your Ideas?'
[194] *A Scandal in Belgravia* (2012).

notion, i.e. when an event, person, idea, or object has no set origin[195]. For *Before the Flood*, the 12th Doctor regales an unseen audience with the tale of a time traveller who loves the work of Ludwig van Beethoven so goes into the past to meet him; however, Beethoven is nowhere to be found. So, worried that the composer's work won't exist, the traveller copies out all the symphonies and publishes them himself under the name Beethoven. So at which point in that closed loop were the compositions created? That sequence has a material consequence, but the point is that such ideas have no beginning.

Doctor Who often uses causal loops in a humorous fashion; for instance, Donna Noble gives Agatha Christie the ideas for Miss Marple and *Murder on the Orient Express* in *The Unicorn and the Wasp* (2008), purely because she's already aware of Christie's work.

However, it's not all fun and games: *Father's Day* (2005) shows the troubles caused if a causal loop is broken, when Rose Tyler saves her father from being run over. Time is only saved when Pete sacrifices himself. (Although the ninth Doctor reckoned he could fix the paradox using the TARDIS, exactly how isn't elaborated on.) This paradox is one reason some believe time travel is impossible: because the outcome would negate the origin of its idea. The go-to thought experiment involves a time traveller murdering Hitler, thus erasing the motivation for the traveller to go back in time to kill

---

[195] *The Black Archive #6: Ghost Light* details the time-loop of Gabriel Chase, the house a young Ace burned down because she sensed an evil presence there – initiated by the Doctor, who investigates the place because Ace burned it down in the future.

Hitler. But if they never killed the dictator, the future would progress as we recognise it, meaning the traveller would go back in time 'again' to kill Hitler.

When Alec Palmer tries to put forth this argument in *Hide* (2013), the 11th Doctor quickly shuts him up by assuring him that the paradoxes resolve themselves, by and large.

In *The Pandorica Opens / The Big Bang*, the Doctor attempted to overcome the ontological paradox by rewriting the notes that directed Amelia to the National Museum; in theory, he could have simply reused the leaflet and the notes Amelia hands him without rewriting, but by doing so, they would have had no physical origin[196]. Nonetheless, the very idea of his positioning Amelia to resurrect Amy and save himself from being trapped inside the Pandorica comes from him already having done those things.

Similarly, we don't know when he thought to reboot the universe using the Pandorica and the exploding TARDIS. The notion was certainly stewing in his mind when he realised that the Dalek had been brought back to life via the light from the box, but after being exterminated, he travelled back in time to meet his past self (again, because he'd already seen this happen), have a whispered exchange, and apparently die. The latter is a lie to give him time to

---

[196] Moffat acknowledged the bootstrap paradox in *Continuity Errors* too, as the seventh Doctor warns his companion, Professor Bernice Summerfield, against reading any of her own future books. She instead asks if she can run copies, to save her time writing them. 'Absolutely not', he replies. 'They come down very heavily on that sort of thing.' Bernice asks if he means the Time Lords, to which he replies, 'Critics.'

work in privacy on his plan. Based on the disappearing exhibits, he wouldn't have been able to initiate the second Big Bang without this additional head-start before the universe entirely blinked out of existence.

Still, we don't know what his future self told his past. It might've been simply an instruction to distract his companions and the Dalek while he was busy. Alternatively, it might've been – if not the whole plan (surely there wasn't time for its entirety) – then at least some choice pointers.

Series 5 also depends on the causal loop that is Amy's memories. To explain why contemporary people in, for instance, *The Invasion* (1968), *Army of Ghosts / Doomsday* (2006), and, later, *Dark Water / Death in Heaven* (2014) didn't recognise the Cybermen after a giant dreadnought trod over Victorian London in *The Next Doctor* (2008), the 11th Doctor posits in *Flesh and Stone* that time had unwritten the event. The implication is that it had been swallowed by the crack: it happened in the Doctor's personal chronology, but was erased from Earth's timeline. The same can be said of the Daleks: they arrived en masse in *Army of Ghosts / Doomsday* and *The Stolen Earth / Journey's End* , yet Amy couldn't remember them in *Victory of the Daleks*.

As the rebooted universe relies on Amy's memories, the only thing that stopped the events of the aforementioned tales from happening is that Amy can't remember them, because they're missing from her memory when she was involved in Big Bang II.

It does leave us with religious questions too. As the TARDIS crew effectively act as deities here, creating a universe from the scraps of the previous one, the concept of a self-perpetuating God could be a solution to that other paradox: if God created us, what created God? Naturally, this is a controversial idea:

> 'because it seemingly negates the "common sense" notion that we are responsible for our own destinies, and, with adequate knowledge and preparation, we can alter their courses. The predestination paradox says the exact opposite, leaving doubt in believers' minds if they really have free will.'[197]

The concept of individuals dancing to the tune of a more powerful force is accurate, however: whether you believe in God or not, we're all dictated to by time. That could be why **Doctor Who** and similar stories that play with time are so attractive: it shows a level of freedom we're not accustomed to, but nonetheless desire. Time isn't a straight line – it can twist out of a seemingly strict shape. It could even be cyclical, which is, of course, an absurd notion. Right...?

The Doctor's Timestream Unravels

> 'I'm rewinding. My time stream unravelling – erasing – closing. Hello, universe. Goodbye, Doctor.'
>
> [The Doctor][198]

And so, we return to time's arrow: a relative concept – relative, that is, to people and places, all across the space-time, according to our proximities to a gravitational force and the limited speed of light. As you approach the speed of light:

---

[197] Hester, Harold, *Heaven's Luck*, p8.
[198] *The Big Bang*.

'time goes slower in the outside world than it does for you. When you hit light speed, the outside world goes so slow in relation to you that it stops (again, in relation to you; people in the outside world feel as if time is the same as always). So if you could push past that speed limit, the outside world would be so slow as to be moving backward in relation to you.'[199]

This causes issues because relativity doesn't give time a direction. Time isn't something that passes; it's something that simply exists.

In this way, we can split our definition of time into two: what we perceive, and what is. Respectively, subjectivity versus objectivity. They're two very different things. Our typical failure to differentiate the two is why we're so surprised black holes eat up time as well as space. We can imagine matter being condensed into a singularity, but struggle to apply the same argument to time, which seemingly doesn't have a beginning or an end. Yet if space and time exist together, as space-time, they're consumed together too.

This is apparently how Steven Moffat views time as well. When in their cross-interview in DWM 551, Russell T Davies suggested that Moffat sees time as 'sort of sentient', Moffat instead compared it to a record on a gramophone, time's progression like a needle. Of course, the record exists in its entirety, but 'you don't know how the song ends while you're still listening, even though the ending is already there.' But that doesn't mean an outcome is inevitable,

---

[199] Pappas, Stephanie, 'Faster-Than-Light Discovery Raises Prospect Of Time Travel.'

solely because you witness it; just that what **appears to be** is inevitable. This again separates subjectivity from objectivity. To demonstrate subjectivity, Moffat noted that the Time War didn't end how the Doctor once perceived it: 'And to the Doctor, it feels like time is being rewritten. But really, it was always that way – he just doesn't know it yet.'[200]

What we perceive is based on repeated patterns. Day turns to night turns to day turns to night. Spring proceeds to summer, giving way to autumn and winter, at which point we return to spring. Once we have repeated patterns, we have a way of marking down our experiences. We'll call this 'time'. These systems rely on Earth's movement around the Sun, and these objects affect what is, i.e. warp time as a wider fabric. It's also surprisingly fragile. Take, for example, the COVID-19 pandemic of 2020 and its subsequent lockdown, which saw people all over the world isolated in their homes and devoid of their daily routines. Unable to leave for work on a regular basis, many found their points of reference were lost.

To demonstrate 'time', Einstein was said to have undertaken an experiment[201] with the abstract, 'When a man sits with a pretty girl for an hour, it seems like a minute. But let him sit on a hot stove for a minute – and it's longer than any hour. That's relativity.' Alas, the universe favours objective time, unaffected by our feelings on the matter – or so it appears. But it's possible that the line between

---

[200] Davies, Russell T, and Steven Moffat, 'Showrunner Showdown.'
[201] He claimed to have published this in the *Journal of Exothermic Science and Technology*; we doubt the accuracy of this, given its acronym. (Zimbardo, Philip, and John Boyd, *The Time Paradox: The New Psychology Of Time That Will Change Your Life*, p339.)

objectivity and subjectivity is blurred, that the continuous motion of time we experience is really the continuous motion of 'time' caused by what we **can** experience. By this proposition, time could consist of disjointed instances that are indistinguishable to us, because we can only experience them in quick procession. Picture them as droplets of water that we're constantly passing through. 'We don't find ourselves slipping from past into future, but rather occupying a present that is itself slipping through time.'[202]

Thermodynamics is the only area of physics that dictates the direction of time. Our perception of time as constantly moving 'forwards' is grounded in entropy, which says that a closed system will naturally gravitate towards disorder. Let's return to that shattered glass on the floor. Those broken pieces won't spontaneously come together again. You can remake the glass with a lot of energy, but it won't be in the exact same state on a molecular level it was before.

Despite its name, the Second Law of Thermodynamics isn't a law science always obeys. It's a rule with exceptions. Technically, it's not impossible for, say, your milk to separate from the water and tea in your cup without a great deal of effort: the chances of it actually happening, however, are so miniscule, none of us will ever see it. It's in that small margin that **Doctor Who** operates. One hypothesis relies on quantum mechanics to reverse the direction of the arrow, i.e. dealing with entanglement, a phenomenon originally described in 1935 in which particles interact and become entwined; no matter how far apart these entangled atoms drift,

---

[202] Clegg, Brian, *Build Your Own Time Machine: The Real Science Of Time Travel*, p63.

108

the properties of one automatically affects the other.

Typical entropy demonstrations note that a cold object cannot transfer energy to further heat a warm object. Heat transfers from something hot to something cold, not the other way around – at least under normal conditions. The change in the cold object will probably be imperceptible, but you'll soon recognise the difference in the formerly hot object.

But in 2017, a team at the Federal University of ABC in São Paulo, Brazil used chloroform – $CHCl^3$, made of one carbon, one hydrogen, and three chlorine molecules – to transfer heat from cold particles towards hotter ones:

> 'The temperature of the hydrogen nucleus was greater than the carbon nucleus. In quantum terms, temperature refers to the probability of the atom's nucleus being in a certain energy state [...] What the scientists saw happen between the two particles over time was the opposite of what you or I can expect in our ordinary lives.'[203]

That is, when the hydrogen and carbon's nuclei entangled (forcibly, achieved by manipulating the nuclei's spin using magnetic resonance[204]), heat flowed backwards.

Time didn't move backwards. However, the Second Law of Thermodynamics was broken on a quantum level. Theories became an actuality. Of course, we'll have to leave it to the Time Lords to

---

[203] Eck, Allison, 'Scientists Reverse Arrow Of Time In Quantum Experiment.'
[204] Micadei, Kaonan, John PS Peterson, et al., 'Reversing The Direction Of Heat Flow In Quantum Correlations.'

do this on a larger scale; nonetheless, if time is determined by entropy, that experiment proves what can be done can also be undone.

Another supposition about time travel involves wormholes, a shortcut through space and time investigated by Einstein and named the Einstein-Rosen Bridge (partly taking its name from Nathan Rosen, a physicist who also advanced the theory). These work on the basis that space-time isn't flat, but is instead littered with wrinkles and voids, and is capable of folding back on itself and linking two sections of the fabric together. On a quantum level, wormholes form, disappear, and reform over and over.

If you could enter a wormhole in one segment of time and emerge in another, it would be possible to travel faster than the speed of light, a determining factor in the direction of time's arrow. But real-life tunnels are a billion-trillion-trillionths of a centimetre across. Still, some scientists consider the possibility of enlarging these to enable humans to pass through.

'Theoretically, a time tunnel or wormhole could do even more than take us to other planets', posited Stephen Hawking[205]. 'If both ends were in the same place, and separated by time instead of distance, a ship could fly in and come out still near Earth, but in the distant past. Maybe dinosaurs would witness the ship coming in for a landing.'

The problem with this is that potential traversers of the Einstein-Rosen Bridge would be trapped inside the wormhole because it would collapse as soon as it's formed. That's where entanglement

---

[205] Hawking, Stephen, 'How To Build A Time Machine.'

on the event horizons of black holes may provide an answer. Remember how entanglement works: no matter how far particles drift from each other, once entangled they remain connected – so much so that tampering with one alters the state of the other[206]. If the particles between two black holes were entangled, with each consuming the radiation the other emits, the antigravitational consequence would stop the wormhole collapsing. There are further issues with that: firstly that we'd have to create black holes that are 'maximally entangled' – we can't create normal black holes, let alone tamper with their quantum compositions – and that:

> 'calculations based on the wormhole types studied so far suggest that using them would actually be slower than simply travelling directly through space [...] The laws of nature seem to insist that wormholes can either perform amazing feats but collapse in an instant, or be traversable but useless.'[207]

Einstein believed nothing could travel faster than light. This ruled out the possibility of quantum entanglement, because it would mean that entangled photons could communicate with each other instantaneously, i.e. faster than time allows[208]. Yet quantum entanglement exists. Further, taking into account the experiment carried out at the Federal University of ABC in São Paulo, and it would appear that time's arrow **can** be broken.

---

[206] See Chapter 6.
[207] Matthews, Robert, 'Through The Wormhole', *BBC Focus* #322.
[208] Clegg, Brian, *Light Years: The Extraordinary Story Of Mankind's Fascination With Light*, p253.

If that's the case, the Doctor's chronology could unravel in a conflicting direction to the rest of time, bringing him closer to his end.

Fortunately, his end is also the beginning.

CHAPTER 6: ENDINGS AND BEGINNINGS

'HELLO SWEETIE ΘΣ Φ ΓΥΔϟ'

[River's graffito][209]

Let's travel back to the beginning – and no, we're not talking about *An Unearthly Child* (1963). Nor are we strictly talking about the beginning of the 11th Doctor era, *The Eleventh Hour*, although we'll come back to that. Instead, we're talking about the Big Bang. The actual one.

As is the nature of finales, *The Pandorica Opens / The Big Bang* plays with the notions of beginnings and endings; notably this is the end for the crack in time arc[210], and the beginning of fresh adventures for the Doctor, Amy and Rory (highlighted further by the intrigue presented by River Song). The series ends with a wedding and them travelling together, Amy wishing the world goodbye and embracing a freedom (and relationships) she loves. There's some friction between Rory and the Doctor in upcoming episodes[211], but as far as contemporary viewers were concerned, the three are now a unit.

At the heart of this theme lie the Pandorica and the TARDIS: both provide the means for the end and the beginning of the universe. Sure, the 'end of everything' is a threat bandied around by all and sundry, but what does that really mean, and how does the Series 5 finale achieve this?

---

[209] *The Pandorica Opens.*
[210] Aside from an encore in *The Time of the Doctor* (2013).
[211] Primarily in *The Impossible Astronaut / Day of the Moon.*

Current scientific understanding is that the universe will continue to expand – more, it will do so at an increasing speed, flying in the face of previous theories on gravity which state that attractions between masses should cause this growth to slow down[212]. Such expansion doesn't mean the universe won't end. Astrophysicist Neil deGrasse Tyson posits that the stars will run out of thermonuclear fuel and die out; while gas clouds will produce new stars, that supply is finite too, so:

> 'you start with gas, you make stars, the stars evolve during their lives, and leave behind a corpse – the dead end-products of stellar evolution: black holes, neutron stars, and white dwarfs. This keeps going until all the lights of the galaxy turn off, one by one. The galaxy goes dark. The universe goes dark. Black holes are left, emitting only a feeble glow of light.'[213]

In *The Pandorica Opens*, however, matter constricts… or appears to. The finale hedges its bets well, not entirely deciding how the universe ends. What we see is roughly in line with the three core theories about its demise.

The first is commonly referred to as 'The Big Rip', which sees expansion continue to a point where it tears atoms apart.

The second idea is of 'The Big Crunch', which imagines that gravity will draw mass together; such has been our understanding of general relativity since Einstein put it forward in 1915 – that large

---

[212] Than, Ker, 'Is Dark Energy Really "Repulsive Gravity"?'

[213] Degrasse Tyson, Strauss, and Gott, *Welcome to the Universe: An Astrophysical Tour*, p24.

bodies cause distortions in space-time, pulling objects towards them, but that the opposite is also true. Gravity is dominant on a local level: that's why our solar system loosely holds itself together[214], why that apple purportedly landed on Isaac Newton's head, and why the Apollo 11 crew bounced around the surface of a smaller celestial body easier than they would have on Earth. 'It's only when you reach hundreds of millions of light-years does the expansion take over from gravity', which further explains why the Andromeda galaxy is heading towards our own at a mind-blowing 110 kilometres per second[215]. The Big Crunch applies this notion to the universe as a whole, whereby expansion means a loss of matter to such an extent that gravity becomes the dominant force.

Think of the 'Big Rip' as the eventual result of an explosion and the 'Big Crunch' as an implosion.

The third hypothesis ties into what deGrasse Tyson describes above as 'Not with a bang, but with a whimper', and the end-point of entropy: the heat death of the universe. This implies a general heating up of the cosmos, yet means the exact opposite. Replace the word 'heat' with 'energy' because this theorises that universal expansion means an even distribution of energy, a finite resource, would mean nothing new could be born. The universe would simply run out of energy to birth new stars, to birth new systems,

---

[214] The Earth drifts about 1.5cm away from the sun every year as the latter loses around 4.7 million tonnes of matter annually, demonstrating that the less mass an object has, the less its gravitational pull. (Siegel, Ethan, 'Earth Is Drifting Away From The Sun, And So Are All The Planets.')
[215] Cain, Fraser, 'Why Is Andromeda Coming Towards Us?'

to birth new life. Time becomes a void in which the future can't be separated from the present as all energy is spent.

If you want to see the effects of entropy, run a bowl of hot water, watch an episode of *Logopolis* (1981), then come back to the bowl 23 minutes later and check its temperature. Apply that loss of heat to everything everywhere.

So how does *The Pandorica Opens / The Big Bang* depict these? *The Big Bang* shows a starless sky, with the very idea of these burning spheres confined to the beliefs of Richard Dawkins and his star cults – presumably consisting of those special individuals who can loosely recall the universe how it was[216], and scientists who recognise how creation should be ordered[217]. A dark sky, bereft of light and life, corresponds with all three aforementioned hypotheses.

From the story's dialogue, too, the audience can draw its own conclusions. Let's first consider the Doctor's warning that 'every sun will supernova at every moment in history.'[218] Supernovas can occur in two ways, the first involving the explosion of a white dwarf (i.e. a spent star) colliding with or drawing too much matter from a nearby star.

---

[216] Notably Amelia.

[217] Let's ruminate that their seeing the exploding TARDIS in the sky led scientists to speculate that the universe is supposed to be filled with similar phenomena. Inferences like that correlate with the Doctor's assertion that you can take the particles from inside the Pandorica and essentially fill in the blanks when it comes to the rest of space-time.

[218] *The Pandorica Opens*.

However, the Doctor is likely alluding to the better-known reason for stars to turn into supernovas: as a sort of 'last hurrah'. Nuclear fission at the heart of a star has incredible outward pressure, but it's confined by its own gravity. As its own energy is depleted, its pressure drops and gravity dominates, causing the mass to collapse in on itself. Despite containing over 99% of all mass in our solar system, our sun is considered a medium-sized star. R136a1, a hypergiant with the greatest known mass, is more than 300 times the size of our sun. Now imagine something that large – or larger still – collapsing in a matter of seconds. The resultant shock waves cause the outer part of the star to explode.

Fortunately, when this happens, 'it briefly (over the course of about a month or so) shines in visible light with a brightness of 10 billion stars. Happily for us, stars don't explode that often, about once per hundred years per galaxy.'[219] We get a visual representation of this at the end of *The Pandorica Opens*: Earth surrounded by the exploding stars of the cosmos. The shot is gorgeous, but causes complications if taken literally.

Consider that those stars uniformly appear to explode at the same instance. Light travels at 186,282 miles per second in a vacuum, meaning light from our sun takes eight minutes and 19 seconds to enter our atmosphere[220]. While it's a myth that all the stars in the night sky are long since dead, some undoubtedly are. The stars seen in the final scene of the episode are either all exactly the

[219] Krauss, p17.
[220] Redd, Nola Taylor, 'How Fast Does Light Travel? The Speed of Light.'

same distance away from Earth[221] or went supernova at different points in time but their light reaches us at the same moment. The latter's a more interesting proposition: the closest star, Proxima Centauri, would still have been 4.22 light-years away[222], so to be seen in 102 CE, it would have exploded around 97 CE. With this in mind, the brightest star in the night sky, Sirius A, 8.6 light-years away, would have gone supernova in 93 CE, and Messier 31 (the furthest you can see with the naked eye)[223], widely known as the Andromeda Galaxy, would have exploded around 2.5 million years before that; at that time on Earth *Homo habilis*, the earliest of our ancestors to show a significant increase in brain size, would have been creating tools to strip meat from scavenged carcasses.

The Doctor's claim, therefore, that stars would supernova 'at every moment in history' doesn't add up, taken at face value. What he probably means is that the stars populating the universe in 102 CE would collapse, and subsequent energies would be expended, i.e. creation experiencing its heat-death.

'Total Event Collapse' could refer to the collapse of these stars. It may also be 'The Big Crunch', applying the logic behind supernovas to the entire cosmos. Alternatively, 'The Big Rip' remains an option as the lack of matter appears to demonstrate that atoms have split apart.

Whatever happened, the sky remains black.

---

[221] We can rule this out as the night sky looked, for all intents and purposes, the same now as it did 2,000 years ago.
[222] Sharp, Tim, 'Alpha Centauri: Closest Star To Earth'.
[223] Clark, Stuart, 'Starwatch: The Furthest Thing You Can See With The Naked Eye.'

And it's not just our reality that's destroyed: as the presence of the Cybus Industries Cybermen demonstrates, not to mention the Cyber-Leader's assertion that 'all universes will be deleted'[224], the TARDIS exploding annihilates the multiverse.

For the purposes of this argument, let's take the existence of a multiverse as a certainty – it's not in reality, but we've seen enough alternate realities in **Doctor Who** to take a multiverse as read. Similarly, how a multiverse would operate in reality is up for question; although **Doctor Who** muddies the water sometimes, there's a clear correlation between cause and effect in the programme. *Orphan 55* (2020) attracted criticism[225] for showing one timeline, one possible future, but something similar occurred in *Pyramids of Mars* (1975), in which the fourth Doctor shows Sarah Jane Smith her future world if they didn't stop Sutekh. Correlate this with *Inferno*, in which the third Doctor travels to a parallel Earth where the consequences of a drilling project are taking their toll. Having glimpsed the future, the Doctor knows the urgency of stopping Project Inferno in his home universe. We could postulate that the possible projections glimpsed in *Pyramids of Mars* and *Orphan 55* are alternate timelines.

This seems to follow the path of the Level III multiverse, the controversial many-worlds hierarchy which suggests timeline splits based on quantum decisions. Picture it as a die being thrown and all outcomes being achievable, albeit split between different realities. In one sixth of the timelines, the die lands on a one; in

---

[224] *The Pandorica Opens.*
[225] Fullerton, Huw, 'Is **Doctor Who** Changing The Rules Of Time Travel?'

another sixth, it lands on a two. Confined to one universe, we can only perceive a singular number[226].

This presents problems for the Cybermen's claim to ring true, assuming, of course, they have the technology to project the outcomes on all parallel worlds. If the TARDIS explodes here, in another universe, it wouldn't explode – that is, unless it does so at a quantum level in this reality, affecting all possible outcomes. To fall back on that dice metaphor, the TARDIS's destruction also obliterates the dice. If they had the capability to predict other multiversal reactions, though, the Cybermen would surely have a smarter method of preventing Total Event Collapse than locking the Doctor in a box. Let's presume the Cybermen were overreaching, inferring that the destruction they calculate in a few universes is indicative of a larger issue. Otherwise, it messes with **Doctor Who**'s multiversal configuration[227].

The notion of a multiverse relies on the aforementioned inflation of the universe, which must occur faster than the speed of light. Matter beyond observable space cannot be influenced, implying an infinite number of other spaces; a universe made of elementary particles – like quarks and leptons, which cannot be broken down further, as far as we're currently aware – can only be constructed

---

[226] Tegmark, Max, 'Parallel Universes: Level III Multiverse', *Scientific American*, Vol. 288, #5.

[227] Interestingly, *Extremis* (2017) largely takes place in a Level IV hierarchy, i.e. a simulation run by the Truth Monks. Still, these aliens are part of the standard **Doctor Who** universe so otherwise play by established rules.

in a set number of configurations[228].

That hypothesis duplicates what happens in our universe with others, whereas *The Pandorica Opens* instead implies that what happens 'here' has a knock-on effect 'there', i.e. everywhere else.

Could the absence of one universe lead to the collapse of the others, like dominoes falling? Aristotle noted that nature abhors a vacuum[229], so when one universe leaves a gap, others rush to fill the void, resulting in multiversal convergence and collapse.

In reality, the Cyber-Leader's statement is probably there solely to shut up that section of fandom who would no doubt complain that the destruction of our universe wouldn't affect the cybernetic beings of 'Pete's World', and so negate a redesign to differentiate the Cybus Industries variations from our own Mondasian or Telosian versions.

So we come back to the crux of the matter: **the sky remains black**.

But a **starless** universe, presumably bereft of life, may not mean an **empty** universe. Using the naked eye, or even powerful optical telescopes, the space between celestial objects is dark. But use radio telescopes to detect different frequencies and you'll see background 'noise'. This includes the strongest in the microwave-

---

[228] 'It's a huge number, 2 to the power of 10^{118}, but since there's no sign that space is finite, there's room for every arrangement to repeat.' (Adler, Robert, 'The Many Faces Of The Multiverse', *New Scientist*, Vol. 212, #2840).
[229] 'The Denser Surrounding Material Continuum Would Immediately Fill The Rarity Of An Incipient Void.' (Wilson, Glynn, 'Nature Abhors a Vacuum: From Aristotle to Thoreau').

radio spectrum: the Cosmic Microwave Background, radiation left over from the universe's creation[230]. 'Does space exist independent of things, in the sense that had I mentally removed all those planes, stars, and assorted pieces of matter, space would remain, or would removal of matter do away with space as well?'[231] What could fill those gaps? The logical conclusion is of a macrocosm consisting of stars' corpses, i.e. either neutron stars or black holes, depending on the star's density.

Although the name 'neutron stars' implies a degree of brightness, much of their energy is emitted as invisible light. These objects of intensely compressed matter are also so small that they're typically ten billion times fainter than anything you can see with the naked eye.[232] It would make sense for regions of space in *The Big Bang* to be made of neutron stars. But what else?

Einstein's theory of general relativity predicted the existence of black holes: the remnant core of a supernova, gravity to the Nth degree, so infinitely dense that nothing can escape – matter, light, not even time. That is, in theory. Professor Stephen Hawking spent much of his life trying to prove that black holes aren't entirely black, that they don't consume **everything**, and that they, too, can end.

2019 was a big year for cosmologists dedicated to researching black holes. Until then, we'd not even seen one. Then, in April that

---

[230] Gunn, Alastair, 'If We Made A Powerful Enough Telescope, Would We Theoretically Be Able To See The Light From The Big Bang?', *BBC Science Focus* #334.
[231] Close, Frank, *Nothing: A Very Short Introduction*.
[232] Miller, Cole, 'Black Holes And Neutron Stars.'

year, the Event Horizon Telescope project, a collaboration of over 200 scientists using a network of eight radio telescopes across the world, unveiled an image of a supermassive black hole in the Messier 87 galaxy, 55 million light years from our planet and with the same mass as 6.5 billion suns. It's what the black hole looked like some 53 million years before humanity existed. An image of a black object in black space wouldn't have been exciting; what came back, though, really was: a whirlpool of light, spiralling out of the dark. **Doctor Who** fans should be familiar with such an image: 'we must give great credit to the visual effects work of The Mill during Series 2, back in 2006, when they designed K37 Gem 5 for *The Impossible Planet* and *The Satan Pit* [(2006)]. The similarity between their work and [the image of Messier 87] is striking.'[233] The depicted light is its accretion disc, super-heated gas emitting radiation on numerous spectrums.

The same year, Jeff Steinhauer and his team at the the Israel Institute of Technology in Haifa modelled an event horizon, i.e. the point of no return for matter on the edge of the dense object's gravitational pull, to prove Hawking was right about black holes emitting particles which siphon off energy, enough to eventually destroy the singularities. Space is partially comprised of matter-antimatter pairings with equal masses but opposing electrical charges. These typically destroy each other, except when the pull of a black hole forces them apart, as one particle is ejected into space (becoming known as Hawking radiation) and the other gets absorbed by the hole. As the latter has negative energy, it reduces

---

Traynier, David, 'First Ever Image of a Black Hole: *The Impossible Planet* Team Got It Right.'

the black hole's heat and mass, eventually leading to its evaporation[234].

The closing of *The Pandorica Opens*, perhaps, leaves us with a universe of collapsed stars reverting to destroyed neutron stars and black holes – or one destroyed black hole that had previously swallowed all the rest[235].

What evidence is there that matter **hasn't** largely vanished, then? It's the impossibility of our visualising 'nothing'. Whenever someone tells us to think of a blank space, we picture either startling white or all-consuming black; neither, however, accurately show nothingness. When mulling over the singularity at the heart of the Big Bang, author Bill Bryson considers, 'outside the singularity, there is no **where**. When the universe begins to expand, it won't be spreading out to fill a larger emptiness. The only space that exists is the space it creates as it goes.'[236] Because there is no space, there cannot be blackness. The singularity at the heart of the Big Bang has nothing around it to occupy. The very fact we can see blackness around Earth is evidence that something else exists.

Of course, our inability to imagine absolute nothingness means the

---

[234] Fore, Meredith, 'Stephen Hawking Was Right: Black Holes Can Evaporate, Weird New Study Shows'.

[235] Black holes with small masses react to the gravitational waves of their larger cousins and are eventually consumed by them. It can take billions of years, but with time also seemingly shrinking, and Earth at its epicentre, apparently disconnected from the wider universe, we can postulate that it occurs swiftly, between scenes, in the Series 5 finale.

[236] Bryson, Bill, *A Short History Of Nearly Everything*, p28.

void is necessarily filled by the dark: the proof that space still exists after Total Event Collapse is only due to television being incapable of showing anything other than that. As far as the Doctor is concerned, 'the universe literally never happened.'[237]

Considering they're not mentioned in the story at all, black holes appear more important to *The Pandorica Opens / The Big Bang* than we might otherwise think. In fact, they could be the blueprint for the Pandorica acting as a singularity, and catalyst for the Big Bang II.

The notion of hope contained in an object may be largely dependent on myth, but if we quantify 'hope' as 'information', it might bear scientific scrutiny too. Black holes present the 'information paradox', meaning that they consume everything and eventually dwindle to nothing, but information, carried by matter and energy, cannot be destroyed. So what happens? Some information could escape through Hawking radiation[238]. Returning to matter-antimatter pairings, when one particle escapes gravitational forces, what's lost to the black hole can be inferred from what remains.

Retrieving information collected by a black hole – and perhaps left in the vacuum generated after a black hole's evaporation – isn't as simple as that (and admittedly deductions based on what **should** be are far from accurate... as evidenced by our changing views on quantum physics). Instead, data collated as quantum bits, known as qubits, is entangled, and we know that, by measuring one

---

[237] *The Big Bang.*
[238] Battersby, *Where The Universe Came From*, p43.

entangled molecule, it forces it, and by extension the other particle it's entangled with, into a fixed state. Any other information the qubit carried would be destroyed by our interference.

Essentially, by fixating on one possibility, it erases its other potentials. Consider Schrödinger's oft-referenced cat, a thought experiment demonstrating quantum superpositioning, in which a feline is sealed in a box with a vial of poison and a radioactive source. If a Geiger counter detects the decay of a single atom, the vial shatters, killing the cat. From an outsider's point of view, the cat is both alive and dead. It's in a superposition. It's only with visual proof that its state is confirmed.

Instead of fixing an entangled molecule, researchers at the Walter Burke Institute for Theoretical Physics tried to calculate the angle and momentum of a particle theoretically thrown into a black hole; to do so, they used an algorithm to record information about said particle, the rotation of the black hole, and the Hawking radiation emitted – then calculate whether the angular momentum had altered. From that, they were able to reverse-engineer the state of the original qubit. The paper's co-author, Adam Jermyn, suggested, 'It's possible the information escapes in the same fashion that, when you delete a file on your computer, technically, the information still exists – it's just been scrambled'.[239]

In **Doctor Who** terms, it's akin to the Cyber-Planner's warning in *Nightmare in Silver* (2013) to the Doctor, who has been systematically deleting himself from databases across space and time: 'You know you could be reconstructed by the hole you've

---

[239] Ghose, Tia, 'How To Teleport Info Out Of A Black Hole'.

left.'

This does fit into *The Pandorica Opens / The Big Bang*'s logic, that you can extract enough information from molecules to infer the rest of the universe. The concept would have been highlighted further by the Doctor in deleted dialogue: 'Now atoms, I love those guys. Every atom tells the story of every other atom.'[240]

It's also in line with the theory of Planck stars, an intensely focussed mass which some postulate sits in the middle of black holes. This is less than a trillionth of a trillionth of a metre, the Planck length, the smallest measurement in physics.

First proposed by Carlo Rovelli and Francesca Vidotto in 2014, Planck stars would contain the sum of all information consumed by the black hole. When the event horizon shrinks towards, and is absorbed by, the Planck star, its information is expelled in what can be described as a 'Big Bounce', spreading its matter and information across space again. It remains a theory – and a controversial one at that – but Vidotto pointed out that it draws on old ideas on black hole mechanics 'but in a really new way that opens up a new direction of research.'[241]

The Pandorica is akin to this bouncing effect, though Planck stars are yet to be observed because, from our viewpoint, larger black holes would take billions of years to initiate such an explosion of matter. If the same can be said of the Big Bang II, the Doctor, being inside the event, witnesses only a short period of this, and the

---

[240] Ainsworth, *Complete History*, Volume 66 p51.
[241] O'Callaghan, Jonathan, 'Strangest Star In The Universe', *All About Space* #100.

TARDIS could equalise the timestreams inside and outside the Pandorica.

If this all sounds mad to you... well, it is. But only as mad as the idea of the Big Bang itself – everything created from a singularity. Something from nothing. **Doctor Who** argues that all you need is a source of infinite power (the TARDIS, capable of transmitting the light from the Pandorica to every particle of space and time simultaneously) and a template. The Pandorica acts as the singularity or Planck star, albeit a rather large one containing a few billion atoms of the universe as it was, perfectly preserved. 'In theory', the Doctor says, 'you could extrapolate the whole universe from a single one of them, like cloning a body from a single cell.'[242]

That template comes from Amy's memories. Information being transmitted by light ties in neatly with the concept of a multiverse existing due to matter outside the **observable** universe, so outside our sphere of influence, as well as the radiation leaking from black holes which contain data.

While the Doctor is put into a god-like position once more[243], Moffat's view of the universe is very human-centric – unsurprising given how he aligns companions at the centre of the show. The Doctor's fascination and love of humanity could have been a driving factor in what would have been his timely unravelling, if it weren't for some choice words with seven-year-old Amelia. The

---

[242] *The Big Bang.*

[243] It's less obvious here than in *Last of the Time Lords* (2007), yet in *The Big Bang*, he **does** become a god – yes, just restoring space and time as they had been beforehand, but he nonetheless creates this matter (with a little help).

Time Lord could have gone to all that effort to restore specifically **our** version of reality. The cosmos has survived without humanity for so long, it could easily do so again. Observations of the Higgs boson suggest we live in a false vacuum, a potential superposition configuration of space-time which shifts between different states but may move from instability to stability. As with Schrödinger's cat, observation of the universe's quantum state could tip it over the edge. This is just a headache-inducing way of saying that reality could disappear, then reappear without humanity[244].

Would the end of creation lead to another universe (or multiverse) being born regardless? It depends on thinking about time as a cyclical entity. Cause and effect dictates life ultimately being extinguished; 'life pushes out the old to make way for the new.'[245]

In considering this, we must question using the Big Bang as the basis for creation, because, quite simply, it doesn't explain a lot of our observations, or lack of them. The size of space, for example, is troublesome. Richard Brent Tully, astronomer at the Institute for Astronomy in Honolulu, Hawaii, found galaxy clusters 300 million light-years long and 100 million light years across, stretched over some billion light years with voids around 300 million light years wide. Because galaxies are moving away from each other at regular speeds,

> 'which is how we calculate the origin of the Big Bang, and at the speed galaxies are moving, these things wouldn't have had time to be created since the Big Bang 10 to 20 billion

---

[244] Brooks, Michael, 'Could We Destroy The Universe?', *New Scientist* Vol. 226, #3019.
[245] Carroll, Sean, 'Ten Things Everyone Should Know About Time'.

years ago. They would have needed at least 80 billion years to have got to this size.'[246]

Astonishingly, they're too big to be explained by the Big Bang.

Black holes can be largely split into two groups: supermassive black holes, each with a mass thousands or billions of times that of our sun; and stellar mass black holes, typically with less than 100 times the mass of the sun. But where are the intermediate mass black holes (IMBHs)? We've no conclusive proof of their existence. That's a problem because astronomers observed supermassive black holes in the first billion years after the Big Bang. Yet there wasn't enough time for them to grow to that size in such a comparatively miniscule amount of time – without them merging from IMBHs[247].

Essentially, there's a lot in the observable universe that isn't explained by the Big Bang. Do we have to stretch our minds further back?

What happened **before** the Big Bang? Obviously, that's one of the great questions to which we're unlikely to find a definitive answer. Nonetheless, it might have something to do with our relationship with time, specifically how we might perceive it in a linear fashion, though it could equally behave cyclically.

Bryson delineates the notion of time and space operating separately, stating that we can't question how long the singularity existed because it was neither there forever nor a microsecond:

---

[246] Osborne, Richard, *The Universe: Explained, Condensed And Exploded*, p103.
[247] Stuart, Colin, 'The Ones That Got Away,' *New Scientist* Vol. 237, #3161.

'Time doesn't exist. There is no past for it to emerge from.'[248]

Cyclical time balks at this, however. Everyone knows Isaac Newton's Third Law of Motion, that, for every action, there is an equal and opposite reaction. What if we applied this to the beginning of the universe? That's the idea behind 'The Big Bounce', which describes expansion as a reaction of a period of rapid contraction, i.e. one universe creating out of another. The cosmos has no beginning; therefore, it has no end.

This Big Bounce is grounded in string theory[249], but don't let that put you off. Imagine our universe is your right hand and your left is another, connected by elastic. You clap, creating a big bang, then draw your hands away. Your hands sting – think of that as energy transference. The stinging subsides, representing the energy expended by pulling your hands apart. The elastic draws your hands together repeatedly. You clap, transferring energy again, right at the point they'd stopped stinging. This bouncing effect produces a lot of big bangs and some very sore palms.

Of course, that's just a theory in which we try to marry quantum theory (the study of the miniscule) with Einstein's universal concept of gravity – seemingly juxtaposing ideas which need unifying to predict how the massive universe operated on a quantum level at its creation, and indeed how it continues to do so.

Then again, if 'the universe literally never happened', perhaps this includes an expansion of space-time before the Big Bang too? We

---

[248] Bryson, p28.
[249] Chown, Marcus, 'What If The Big Bang Was Not The Beginning?', *BBC Science Focus* #334.

don't know whether creation is a given. Did the Doctor effect Big Bang II unnecessarily? We don't know that either, and it will probably be quite a while before we find out. Just be glad he did.

And that leaves us with one question: why is 26 June 2010 the 'base code of the universe'[250], not around 13.75 billion years ago[251] or Easter 1996, when Amelia visits the National Museum?

The Doctor's statement is ambiguous. Is that date when the universe actually began again? Or is it **displayed** by River's scanner as written in the base code? There's further ambiguity here, because River can't read the base code, so asks the Doctor to explain. Bear in mind that the TARDIS's translation circuits probably converted readings from the crack in time into a knowable quantity, i.e. partially based on a mathematical equation, but also the Gregorian calendar. We assume the base code is akin to the codebase used in software development, meaning a collection of sources used to build something greater. 26 June 2010 might be a simplified version, which nonetheless has some significance to the arc and warns the Doctor when the TARDIS will be destroyed. So why is that?

Narratively, it's because that's when the TARDIS blows up. True, the explosion caused the cracks in time; with those sealed, the TARDIS never exploded. Except it was that explosion that fuelled the Big Bang II, rebooting the universe. We're stuck in that paradox again – fitting for such a timey-wimey tale. In a meta way, the base code reads the date on which *The Big Bang* was initially

---

[250] Various episodes, but firstly in *Flesh and Stone*.
[251] Webb, Richard, 'The Dating Game'. *New Scientist* #2833.

transmitted. But there's a more important reason for 26 June 2010's inclusion – and, typical to Moffat's writing, it focuses squarely on Amy Pond and her reliance on the Doctor, and ties together the series beautifully. Amy's wish is realised, giving credence to the 'dreams can come true' adage. The Doctor isn't just an imaginary friend anymore, and Rory isn't simply an idealistic relationship, because Amy 'has finally woven the disparate elements of her life together. Her husband watches her friend do the Drunk Giraffe dance. She doesn't have to choose anymore.'[252]

Aside from the date's importance as the day of her and Rory's wedding, it's also the day the universe is properly completed in its current form. Those gaps in history left by the Doctor's absence are filled in. It's also when Amy's life makes some semblance of sense and when the first marked change in her character is complete. Her initial meeting with the man who falls out of the sky and eats fish fingers and custard warps her expectations; she becomes distrustful, believing the Doctor is a liar who left her to fend for herself. Series 5 details the journey back to her original, more optimistic state of mind. 'And that's what [the Doctor] does: by the end, she's capable of standing up at the wedding and actually believing all of that was real. "Raggedy Man, I remember you" - that's what it's all about', Steven Moffat explained to **Doctor Who Confidential**[253]. 'He puts her back, in a way, to the heart and the spirit and the soul of the girl he first met, who he so damaged by being a little tad late.'

---

[252] Brice-Bateman, Liam, 'Reviewed: **Doctor Who** Series 5 – Brighter Than Sunflowers.'
[253] *Out of Time.*

Essentially, if we split the Ponds' adventures with the Doctor into three eras – loosely, a beginning, middle, and end – then *The Big Bang* is the end of the first era, *The God Complex* (in which Amy's loss of faith in the Doctor echoes Series 5, before he once more restores it) concludes their second era, and *The Angels Take Manhattan* (2012) is definitively the end. Amy doesn't lose faith in the Doctor in Series 7, but she and Rory nevertheless become disillusioned with the life they'd led for 10 years, and eventually, she saves herself by escaping to a set time period with her husband.

The cyclical nature of Series 5 would have been added to further if the intended final shot of *The Big Bang*, the ducks finally returned to their duck pond in Leadworth, hadn't have been abandoned due to shifting filming locations. Fortunately, the Doctor's moved his TARDIS to Amy's back garden – better parked, it has to be said, than his initial landing in *The Eleventh Hour* – so the audience undoubtedly get the message.

The end and the beginning. The Doctor, Amy, and Rory, time and time again. That's what *The Pandorica Opens / The Big Bang* is about.

CONCLUSION

'Sorry, something's come up. This will have to be goodbye.'

[The Doctor][254]

As a **Doctor Who** fan, you're not supposed to have a favourite Doctor, at least not one you'd publicly reveal. Concessions are allowed, however, for having an incarnation considered as 'my Doctor', i.e. the one you grew up with, who aligns with your idea of the lead character the most, or who helped you through a particularly difficult time.

I think the same rule applies to favourite stories. You're not supposed to have one. After all, with so much history, so many creative teams, and narratives spanning different genres, how could you pick **just one**? But most of us do. There's that sole tale that particularly resonates with you, that makes you laugh and cry, that means just that little bit more than all the rest. Put aside what you hear online: most **Doctor Who** fans actually like **Doctor Who**. I adore *The Tomb of the Cybermen*, *The Robots of Death* (1977), and *Smile* (2017). I love vast swathes of the programme. Nonetheless, I'm happy to break that unspoken rule and announce *The Pandorica Opens / The Big Bang* as my favourite **Doctor Who** story. I hope it's now evident why.

When David Tennant left the role of the 10th Doctor, I was apprehensive about the new guy – the one with the ridiculous hair. Then he burst out of the TARDIS and asked for an apple and I knew he'd be good. By the end of *The Eleventh Hour*, he simply **is** the

---

[254] *The Big Bang.*

Doctor.

Actually, my first glimpse of Smith's Doctor was before that: I saw his first scene – the TARDIS crashing, the Doctor just missing Big Ben, the TARDIS ricocheting through the air – in 3D on a big screen in Plymouth. It was on a loop, but I was transfixed anyway. I was excited. The apprehension abated swiftly as a new era of my favourite show dawned. That was on 3 April 2010: we dashed back to the annex we were holidaying in so we could watch *The Eleventh Hour* on transmission. I was also lucky enough to interview Matt Smith at the *Doctor Who Experience* in October 2012 and he was exactly what you'd expect from the Doctor: funny, thoughtful, and very giving of his time. Forget that 'never meet your heroes' nonsense. The exhibition was the perfect place to reflect on how big **Doctor Who** was. As I write this, 10 years on from *The Pandorica Opens / The Big Bang*'s initial airing, it's incredible to consider how memorable the iconography of Series 5 remains. Casual fans fondly recall the crack in time and the Pandorica. Vincent van Gogh's *The Pandorica Opens* painting influences the Complete Fifth Series steelbook (2020) cover by artist Sophie Cowdrey; can be found as a print by GB Posters; and is emblazoned on a scarf by Lovarzi. **Doctor Who** isn't a quaint little franchise; it's big and recognisable and much-loved.

And yet it's personal to each of us. We all have a special relationship with it. And that is exemplified by the Series 5 finale, which manages to be 'big and little at the same time, brand new and ancient'.

Not bad for a series about a madman in a box, eh…?

APPENDIX: 'GOOD QUESTION FOR ANOTHER DAY.'[255]

AMY

What, something's going to happen to the TARDIS?

RIVER

It might not be that literal.[256]

Oh my dear River, you have been naïve. The TARDIS explodes and takes the universe with it. What a way to go. Except this raises a lot of questions that are never fully answered in **Doctor Who**.

Principally, we don't know who exactly blew up the TARDIS, why, or how. The strands begin to unpick across Series 6 and 7, culminating in *The Time of the Doctor*, in which we finally find out the details. Sort of.

'I thought I'd left the bath running', quips the Doctor, and that satisfies the core audience members who have distant memories of the TARDIS's destruction a few years prior and, because it doesn't affect the narrative of the Christmas special in any way, are content to know that it was an attempt to stop the Doctor getting to Trenzalore. More recently, we've seen the aftermath of this battle: a planet-wide graveyard in *The Name of the Doctor*. You can see why parties would want to avert this. There's also a mention of River Song and it's clear that the 11th Doctor era has all been leading to his final adventure. Neat. Get the champagne out: we're

---

[255] *The Big Bang.*
[256] *The Pandorica Opens.*

celebrating Steven Moffat's brilliantly immersive and layered approach to storytelling.

But the fizz went to our heads. While the casual viewers woke up on Boxing Day with a warm feeling of satisfaction, fans took to the internet to find answers to lingering questions. Namely:

- How did the TARDIS blow up?
- Who was the voice in the TARDIS at the end of *The Pandorica Opens*?

Steven Moffat left his showrunner position with *Twice Upon A Time*, so it appears that these questions will never be fully answered and you'll have to live with that. However, we can explore what we **do** know and infer the rest...

Who blew up the TARDIS and why? 'The Kovarian Chapter broke away,' explains Tasha Lem. 'They travelled back along your timeline and tried to prevent you ever reaching Trenzalore.' How effective is this? As both Lem and the Doctor point out: not remotely. In fact, the destiny trap dictates that you can't change history if you're part of it, so Madame Kovarian and her brethren 'created the very cracks in the universe through which the Time Lords are now calling'[257]. Nonetheless, their goal is to stop the Doctor getting to Trenzalore so he can't stand as its protector and potentially bring back the Time Lords.

They do so in a thorough fashion. They plan on killing the Doctor by engineering his own bespoke psychopath to shoot him at a fixed point in time, and by blowing up the TARDIS. You'd think only the

---

[257] *The Time of the Doctor* (2013).

former would be necessary, but their belt-and-braces approach perhaps derives from something the Daleks say.

The Supreme Dalek states that 'only the Doctor can pilot the TARDIS'[258] – which seems naïve. But it's a fair assertion if we consider that, while we've seen numerous others at the metaphorical wheel, none of the Alliance have. Some might have inferred that other people could do so, but there's enough evidence to suggest to them that those individuals weren't around.

We can say, definitively, that it's not just the Doctor who can pilot the TARDIS, though the number of individuals who can is minimal[259]. The only people who are **really good** at controlling the TARDIS are the Time Lords. As far as the Daleks are concerned, the Time Lords are all dead[260], ergo removing the Doctor from the situation is probably a fair reaction.

Presumably one of the Silents has been on the TARDIS at some point, and likely reported back to Kovarian that others can steer it. And don't forget that the Church of the Papal Mainframe know something the Alliance don't: the Time Lords are alive and pushing to get back into the correct universe. The Kovarian Chapter may

---

[258] *The Pandorica Opens*.

[259] River Song, for example, pilots the Type 40 TT to 26 June 2010, albeit unwillingly, although few have seen her at the controls.

[260] We're postulating that the Daleks haven't time-travelled back from Trenzalore, so don't know that Gallifrey was saved. After *Victory of the Daleks*, the Paradigm intended to 'return to [their] own time and begin again' via a Time Corridor. Their chronology seems to follow that of the 11th Doctor era, meaning *The Pandorica Opens* occurs after *Victory* but before *The Time of the Doctor*.

worry that the almighty race could remotely control the TARDIS. Certainly they can influence events in this universe from another – they do so to reopen the structural weakness in the wall and the sky over Trenzalore, and to give the Doctor a new regenerative cycle.

Given this, the decision not just to kill the Doctor, but also destroy his ship, is completely understandable.

Whose voice do we hear over the TARDIS tannoy? Contemporary accounts showed how grand (and tied into the show's own mythology) expectations were:

> 'The Black Guardian? Davros? A future iteration of the Doctor? Perhaps even, given how well *The Pandorica Opens* linked back to the rest of the series, it's something to do with Prisoner Zero back in *The Eleventh Hour* (we strongly think that Prisoner Zero, or his captors, have a big part to play with all of this)? Perhaps even Omega if you want to dig back into Old **Who** still further?'

Further names thrown into the mix included the Dream Lord[261], the Master, and the Rani. Think of a **Doctor Who** character, however obscure and tenuous, and someone will have suggested it. Susan? Drax? Adric…? Suffice to say, the actual answer – 'probably a member of the Kovarian chapter' – wouldn't have gone down so well, especially given we'd yet to meet the architects of the TARDIS's destruction.

Prisoner Zero's potential involvement is an interesting notion,

---

[261] Brew, Simon, 'Trying To Answer The Questions Raised By **Doctor Who**: *The Pandorica Opens*'.

however. The crack in Amelia's wall linked our world to what appears to be the Atraxi's prison; Rosanna Calvierri confirmed that 'through some [cracks], we saw worlds and people, and through others, we saw Silence and the end of all things'[262], so the time fields definitely act as wormholes, connecting two different locations. This isn't to say, though, that Prisoner Zero has anything to do with the Papal Mainframe. Instead, he's likely heard the mantra that the Pandorica will open and silence will fall.

Perhaps the notion of wormholes hints at how duality played a part in the TARDIS's demise...

So what exactly caused the TARDIS to explode? There's no 'How to Destroy Your TARDIS' Manual that we know about, and even if there were, the Doctor probably would have disagreed with it and thrown it into a supernova – just as he did with the real TARDIS Instruction Manual[263]. Still, the ship has apparently been destroyed before and since, so it's not as rare an event as you might think.

Journey to the Centre of the TARDIS, for instance, features it blowing up after the Doctor shuts its defences back to basic. Caught in the path of a magno-grab, the resulting magnetic hobble-field caused the heart of the capsule to explode; presumably only the TARDIS's consciousness survived enough to envelop the ensuing explosion and so temporarily save the Doctor and Clara[264].

---

[262] *The Vampires of Venice.*

[263] He admits this in *Amy's Choice*. We'd previously seen it in *The Pirate Planet* (1978), *The Horns of Nimon* and *Vengeance on Varos* (1985). The 2007 animation, *The Infinite Quest* confirms that the 10th Doctor still owned the Manual.

[264] Similar to its sealing off the control room and placing it in a time

The radiation that caused the discharge could have been averted by shield oscillators, which the Doctor had deactivated. This tells us that a) the TARDIS can be destroyed through outside interference; and b) just like the Pandorica, it has layers of security which can be deactivated.

The TARDIS faced catastrophe in *Amy's Choice*, from a star burning cold and freezing the vessel's instruments, and from the Doctor activating the self-destruct protocols. Admittedly, it's just a dream world, but it's as accurate as possible in an effort to fool the Doctor. This tells us that the TARDIS can self-destruct. That opens the possibility that that's exactly what happened. You'd need someone operating the console to do this – and that's where River comes in. The Doctor's dedicated assassin who falls in love with him wouldn't do it on purpose; however, the Silents manipulate people through post-hypnotic suggestion. So, while River was at the controls of the TARDIS, could she have been subconsciously obeying latent instructions from her original programming? Even if she didn't activate the procedure to detonate the ship, she could have lowered defences back to basic, so an external force could destroy it.

Yet we're told numerous times in the programme's history that nothing can get into the TARDIS. Once inside, the Doctor and companions are safe; the ninth Doctor assures Rose that 'the assembled hordes of Genghis Khan couldn't get through those doors – and believe me, they've tried.'[265] Similarly, nothing seems to penetrate the TARDIS defences.

---

loop to save River.
[265] *Rose.*

Well, that's not quite true. A transmat beam does exactly that in *Bad Wolf*, albeit a beam 'fifteen million times more powerful' than a standard one. Sutekh's will extends inside the TARDIS in *Pyramids of Mars* (1975); gravitational dissonance separates the external dimensions from the internal dimension in *Frontios*; a spambot penetrates the ship's defences to advertise the Psychic Circus in *The Greatest Show in the Galaxy* (1988- 89); Donna is accidentally pulled inside by the magnetisation of distant huon particles in *The Runaway Bride*; a *Kerblam!* (2018) Man delivers a fez directly to the 13th Doctor; and the Kasaavin phase through the doors in *Spyfall*. The Daleks certainly have the power. We can presume they learnt a few things about Time Lord technology during the Time War. While additional shielding from the tribophysical waveform macro-kinetic extrapolator fends off the Daleks in *The Parting of the Ways*, the 10th Doctor laments that, against a fully-fledged Dalek Empire at the height of its power, the wooden doors **are** just wood. We later witness the Daleks' attempt at destroying the TARDIS in *Journey's End* as it plummets into a ball of Z-neutrino energy in the Crucible's core. Then, in *The Magician's Apprentice / The Witch's Familiar*, their methods are refined further: they aim a souped-up gun at it and it apparently implodes; it's actually dispersed by the Hostile Action Displacement System, but the Daleks still believed this would work.

What's certain is that the TARDIS can be destroyed by outside forces. But that isn't to say that's what definitely happened.

What the Doctor defines himself as in *Flesh and Stone* must also be true of the TARDIS: that it's a complicated space-time event. As is the nature of *The Pandorica Opens / The Big Bang*, we could hypothesise that a paradox is involved. The TARDIS is better at obeying the laws of time than the Doctor: that's why it puts up such a fuss at his journeying to Trenzalore prematurely in *The Name of the Doctor*, gets him to Utah ready for his apparent death in Series 6, and stops the 12th Doctor going back too far in *Before the Flood*.

As all predictions confirm that the TARDIS will blow up, does the ship paradoxically force this on itself, unable to escape the fixed point (safe in the knowledge that the Doctor will find a way around it)?

If Series 5 had followed its original plan, *The Doctor's Wife*[266] would have made it clear that the TARDIS knew about its imminent demise. At the end of Neil Gaiman's initial draft, the Doctor realises that 'there's only one thing that could crack the whole of time and space when it blows up... The TARDIS. When she blows. And she knew it too.'[267] This would likely have replaced the Doctor reaching into the crack at the conclusion of *Cold Blood* and retrieving a splinter of the TARDIS exterior.

If that's too much of a stretch for your sensibilities, some fans found greater significance in the double-doored TARDIS in Van Gogh's painting: could the TARDIS have collided with another – or indeed itself? The Eye of Harmony works by trapping a star on the verge of its descent into a supernova or black hole; both of these incredibly heavy objects have an immense effect on gravity and, as such, curve space-time, allowing access to different periods. Thanks to the existence of Hawking radiation, we know that black

---

[266] The episode was delayed until Series 6, apparently for budgetary reasons.

[267] Gaiman, Neil, Twitter, April 2020.

holes don't entirely consume but also emit: this partially solves the aforementioned 'information paradox', which states that nothing can escape a black hole but that information cannot be destroyed. Wormholes, however, may give us another answer, as some scientists believe event horizons are riddled with wormholes that allow information to escape alongside the energy emitted by Hawking radiation[268].

These Einstein-Rosen Bridges may link two entangled particles, and therefore could hold the key to time travel, as previously discussed. If the TARDIS operates similarly on a quantum level, its entanglement with particles in other spaces or times would affect what happens to the TARDIS. As its interior is its own dimension, perhaps those particles are entangled with themselves at a different point in time – that is, when the TARDIS explodes.

The idea that the TARDIS explodes because the TARDIS explodes is an intriguing possibility, entirely fitting with the themes of the narrative, i.e. self-perpetuating events. For instance, Amy only restores a version of the universe that she remembers; what she doesn't, paradoxically can't come back because she doesn't remember it in the first place. In that respect, the TARDIS could have been affected by the restored universe: it explodes because Amy knows that's what happens. The details remain fuzzy because she wasn't there at its combustion; nevertheless, the TARDIS could have conformed to the simple memory.

We do at least know that the TARDIS is affected by its environment, from the small – the internal dimension shakes when

---

[268] Matthews, 'Through The Wormhole.'

the Sontarans move it in *The Poison Sky* – to the large, like its state in *The Edge of Destruction*: the Fast Return Switch turned the crew on each other and heated up the internal workings as the ship travelled backwards to the start of time.

How could a new universe affect the previous? Though you might argue it hinges on the concept of cyclical time,

> 'a cyclical disruption of cause and effect would create such an immense feedback loop that it would basically break, uh, all of time and space. For the big brains, breaking time and space may be the most impossible paradox of them all: If you break all of time and space, you'd erase the event that broke time and space in the first place which meant that time and space would never be broken, until it broke again.'[269]

This paradox could be reconciled when the universe is rebooted.

In *Castrovalva* (1982), Event One, aka the original Big Bang, poses a threat, so that's certainly capable of destroying the TARDIS. Might the eruption of Big Bang II have released such a wave of energy, it travelled backwards in time to the previous universe[270], focussing that power on the remaining heavy space-time object, the TARDIS, causing it to explode?

And there we are. Six potential reasons the TARDIS blew up:

- The Kovarian Chapter had a really big gun.

---

[269] Kilson, Kashann, 'Dr Who And The Bootstrap Paradox Is Sci-Fi Time Travel With Actual Physics'.
[270] *The Fires of Pompeii* established that a big enough eruption can form a rupture in time and affect the past.

- River did it subconsciously on the instructions of the Silents, by either activating the self-destruct controls or by stripping them down to basic mode so an external force could attack.
- The TARDIS was caught in a paradox, obeying the fixed point in time that decrees it **must** destroy itself in order to create the cracks in time that brought it, the Doctor, Amy, Rory, and River to be where they are.
- The TARDIS's molecules, as a result of its travels through space-time, were maximally entangled with a time-displaced version of itself, i.e. earlier or later in its personal chronology, which detonated. This quantum entanglement forced the TARDIS to reflect the particles at the point of destruction.
- The Big Bang II resulted in such an incredible discharge of energy that it temporarily affected the previous space-time fabric, igniting the TARDIS and causing the very explosion that resulted in the Big Bang II.
- The TARDIS blew up because Amy remembered it had blown up. With the cracks soaking up her memories, and the universe restored based on her recollections, the TARDIS blew up because we know it blew up.

Pick one. It's entirely up to you which you choose. Fittingly, you can even pick two. Or none of them. Wait for the potential Target novelisation for another definitively indefinitive reason. In true superposition fashion, all of those suppositions are correct and all are false.

Because the biggest question of all isn't about how the TARDIS blew up. It never was. That's a mere technicality. We got enough answers to allow us to carry on with our lives largely uninterrupted.

The biggest question of all: does it really matter...? The important thing was that Steven Moffat wanted to tell a story. More than that, he wanted to make it a good one.

And it was, you know. It was the best.

BIBLIOGRAPHY

Books

Arnold, Jon, *The Eleventh Hour*. **The Black Archive** #19. Edinburgh, Obverse Books, 2018. ISBN 9781909031685.

Barr, Jason, and Camille DG Mustachio, ed, *The Language Of Doctor Who: From Shakespeare To Alien Tongues*. London, Rowman & Littlefield, 2014. ISBN 9781442234802.

Battersby, Stephen, ed, *Where The Universe Came From*. Great Britain, John Murray Learning, 2017. ISBN 9781473629592.

Bettelheim, Bruno, *The Uses Of Enchantment: The Meaning And Importance Of Fairy Tales*. London, Penguin Books, 1991. ISBN 9780140137279.

Booker, Christopher, *The Seven Basic Plots: Why We Tell Stories*. London, Continuum Books, 2004. ISBN 9780826480378.

Bryson, Bill, *A Short History Of Nearly Everything*. Third ed, London, Transworld Publishers, 2016. ISBN 9781784161859.

Burk, Graeme, and Robert Smith?, *Who Is The Doctor: The Unofficial Guide To Doctor Who*. Toronto, Canada, ECW Press, 2012. ISBN 9781550229844.

Christie, Agatha, *Murder On The Orient Express*. Facsimile ed, Harper Collins, 2006. ISBN 9780008226664

Clegg, Brian, *Build Your Own Time Machine: The Real Science Of Time Travel*. London, Duckworth Overlook, 2011. ISBN 9780715645185.

Clegg, Brian, *Light Years: The Extraordinary Story Of Mankind's*

Fascination With Light. Third ed, London, Icon Books, 2015. ISBN 9781848318144.

Close, Frank, *Nothing: A Very Short Introduction*. New York, Oxford University Press Inc., 2009. ISBN 9780199225866.

Collins, Frank, *The Pandorica Opens: Exploring The Worlds Of The Eleventh Doctor*. Cambridge, Classic TV Press, 2011. ISBN 9780956100023.

Conan Doyle, Arthur, *A Study In Scarlet*. London, Penguin Books, 2008. ISBN 9780141034331.

Cooper, Stuart, and Kevin Mahoney, *Steven Moffat's Doctor Who 2010: The Critical Fan's Guide To Matt Smith's First Series*. London, Punked Books, 2011. ISBN 9780953317295.

Cornell, Paul, *Human Nature*. **Doctor Who: The New Adventures**. London, Virgin Books, 1995. ISBN 9780426204433.

Davies, Russell T, *Damaged Goods*. **Doctor Who: The New Adventures**. London, Virgin Books, 1996. ISBN 9780426204831.

Degrasse Tyson, Neil, Michael Strauss, and Richard A Gott, *Welcome To The Universe: An Astrophysical Tour*. Oxfordshire, Princeton University Press, 2016. ISBN 9780691157245.

Dennis, Jonathan, *Ghost Light*. **The Black Archive** #6. Edinburgh, Obverse Books, 2016. ISBN 9781909031432.

Frankel, Valerie Estelle, *Doctor Who And The Hero's Journey: The Doctor And Companions As Chosen Ones*. Unknown, CreateSpace, 2016. ISBN 9781523461042.

Franz, Marie-Louise von, *The Interpretation Of Fairy Tales*. Massachusetts, Shambhala Publications Inc, 1996. ISBN

9780877735267.

Flieger, Verlyn, and Douglas A Anderson, *Tolkien On Fairy-Stories*. London, Harper Collins, 2014. ISBN 9780007582914.

Garfield, Simon, *Timekeepers: How The World Became Obsessed With Time*. Edinburgh, Canongate Books, 2016. ISBN 9781782113195.

Hesiod, *Works And Days*. AE Stallings, trans, London, Penguin Classics, 2018. ISBN 9780141197524.

Hester, Harold, *Heaven's Luck*. Sterling House, 2001. ISBN 9780557601790.

Hickman, Jonathan, et al, *Secret Wars*. Marvel, 2016. ISBN 9781846536892.

Hickman, Jonathan, et al, *Avengers: Time Runs Out*. Marvel, 2016. ISBN 9780785198093.

Joyce, James, *Ulysses*. Hertfordshire, Wordsworth Editions, 2010. ISBN 9781840226355.

Krauss, Lawrence M, *A Universe From Nothing*. London, Simon & Schuster, 2012. ISBN 9781471112683.

Osborne, Richard, *The Universe: Explained, Condensed And Exploded*. Third ed, Harpenden, Pocket Essentials, 2016. ISBN 9780857301161.

Richards, Justin, and Andy Lane, eds, *Decalog 3: Consequences*. **Doctor Who**. London, Virgin Books, 1996. ISBN 9780426204786.

Scott, Cavan, and Mark Wright, *Who-Ology: The Official Miscellany*. BBC Books, 2013. ISBN 9781849906197.

Shields, David, *Reality Hunger: A Manifesto*. London, Penguin Books, 2011. ISBN 9780141049076.

Tatar, Maria, ed, *The Cambridge Companion To Fairy Tales*. Cambridge, Cambridge University Press, 2015. ISBN 9781107634879.

Tribe, Steve, *Doctor Who: The TARDIS Handbook*. BBC Books, 2010. ISBN 9781846079863.

Verdet, Jean-Pierre, and Anthony Zielonka, *The Sky: Order And Chaos*. London, Thames and Hudson, 1992. ISBN 9780500300213.

Woods, Naomi, *Mrs Hemingway*. London, Picador, 2015. ISBN 9781447226888.

Zimbardo, Philip, and John Boyd, *The Time Paradox: The New Psychology Of Time That Will Change Your Life*. New York, Free Press, 2009. ISBN 9781416541998.

Zipes, Jack, *The Irresistible Fairy Tale: The Cultural And Social History Of A Genre*. Oxfordshire, Princeton University Press, 2012. ISBN 9780691159553.

Periodicals

BBC Science Focus (formerly *BBC Focus*), BBC Magazines, 1992-.

Chown, Marcus, 'What If The Big Bang Was Not The Beginning?', *BBC Science Focus* #334, April 2019.

Gunn, Alastair, 'If We Made A Powerful Enough Telescope, Would We Theoretically Be Able To See The Light From The Big Bang?', *BBC Science Focus* #334, April 2019.

Matthews, Prof. Robert, 'Through The Wormhole'. *BBC*

Focus #322, June 2018.

Doctor Who Magazine (DWM), Panini Comics, 1979-.

Davies, Russell T, and Steven Moffat 'Showrunner Showdown.' DWM #551, cover date June 2020.

Moore, Steve, and Dave Gibbons, *The Life Bringer!*. DWM #49-50, cover dates February to March 1981.

Spilsbury, Tom, ed, 'Review: *The Pandorica Opens / The Big Bang*'. DWM #424, cover date 18 August 2010.

New Scientist, Reed Business Information (RBI), 1956-.

Adler, Robert, 'The Many Faces Of The Multiverse', *New Scientist* vol 212, #2840, 26 November 2011.

Amit, Gilead, 'How Did Reality Get Started?' *New Scientist* vol 245 #3267, 1 February 2020.

Battersby, Stephen, 'The End Of Time'. *New Scientist* vol 212, #2833, 8 October 2011.

Brooks, Michael, 'Could We Destroy The Universe?', *New Scientist* vol 226, #3019, 2 May 2015.

Brooks, Michael, 'Here. There. Everywhere?' *New Scientist* vol 246 #3280, 2 May 2020.

Stuart, Colin, 'The Ones That Got Away,' *New Scientist* vol 237, #3161, 20 January 2018.

Ainsworth, John, ed, *Doctor Who: The Complete History – Volume 66* (2017).

Bartlett, RC, 'An Introduction To Hesiod's *Works And Days*', The

Review of Politics Vol. 68, #2, Spring 2006.

O'Callaghan, Jonathan, 'Strangest Star In The Universe,' *All About Space* #100, February 2020.

Tegmark, Max, 'Parallel Universes: Level III Multiverse', *Scientific American*, Vol. 288, #5, May 2003.

Television

Doctor Who. BBC, 1963-.

Doctor Who: The Complete Fifth Series. Blu-ray release, 2010.

The Big Bang: In-Vision Commentary.

The Eleventh Hour: In-Vision Commentary.

Doctor Who Confidential. BBC, 2005-11.

Alien Abduction, 2010.

Out of Time, 2010.

Once Upon A Time. ABC, 2011-18.

Press Gang. ITV, 1989-93.

Star Trek: Voyager. UPN, 1995-2001.

Message in a Bottle, 1998.

The Sarah Jane Adventures. BBC, 2007-11.

Death of the Doctor, 2010.

The Simpsons. 20th Century Fox, 1989-.

Treehouse of Horror VI, 1995.

Mountain of Madness, 1997.

Torchwood. BBC, 2006-11.

Film

Donner, Richard, dir, *The Goonies*. Warner Bros., 1985.

Spielberg, Steven, dir, *Raiders of the Lost Ark*. Lucasfilm Ltd., 1981.

Web

'**Doctor Who** Exclusive: Matt Smith Is A Hit With Children And Middle Classes'. *Radio Times*, 27 September 2011. https://www.radiotimes.com/news/2011-09-27/doctor-who-exclusive-matt-smith-is-a-hit-with-children-and-middle-classes/. Accessed 22 December 2018.

'Fairy-tale'. The Cambridge Dictionary, date unknown, https://dictionary.cambridge.org/dictionary/english/fairy-tale. Accessed 18 August 2019.

'It's Never Over With **Doctor Who**'. *Waikato Times*, 20 April 2013. http://www.stuff.co.nz/waikato-times/life-style/8576237/Its-never-over-with-Doctor-Who. Accessed 17 August 2019.

'Public Domain Artifact Aka: Pandora's Box.' *TV Tropes*. https://tvtropes.org/pmwiki/pmwiki.php/Main/PublicDomainArtifact. Accessed 5 November 2018.

'Steven Moffat On Matt Smith's Era, Writing The 50th Anniversary And More'. **Doctor Who: The Fan Show**. *YouTube*, 17 January 2018. https://www.youtube.com/watch?v=ZOfIIqb8Uhg. Accessed 6 November 2018.

Ailes, Emma, 'Terrifying Time Loop: The Man Trapped In Constant

Déjà Vu.' *BBC News*, 24 January 2015.
https://www.bbc.co.uk/news/uk-30927102. Accessed 26
November 2018.

Becker, Rachel A, '4 Ways Polar Bears Are Dealing With Climate
Change.' *National Geographic*, 4 September 2015.
https://www.nationalgeographic.com/news/2015/09/150904-
polar-bears-dolphins-seals-climate-change/. Accessed 2 February
2020.

Billen, Andrew, '**Doctor Who** Saves The World, Again. Yawn.' *The
Times*, 2 April 2010. https://www.thetimes.co.uk/article/doctor-
who-saves-the-world-again-yawn-sjg56d3rhl5. Accessed 23
February 2020.

Boyle, Rebecca, 'In Test of Relativity Theory, Superaccurate Atomic
Clocks Prove Your Head Ages Nanoseconds Faster than Your Feet.'
Popular Science, 24 September 2010.
https://www.popsci.com/science/article/2010-09/superaccurate-
clocks-prove-your-head-older-your-feet/. Accessed 14 March 2019.

Brew, Simon, 'Trying To Answer The Questions Raised By **Doctor
Who**: *The Pandorica Opens*.' *Den of Geek*, 21 June 2010.
https://www.denofgeek.com/tv/doctor-who/20491/trying-to-
answer-the-questions-raised-by-doctor-who-the-pandorica-opens.
Accessed 28 January 2020.

Brice-Bateman, Liam, 'Reviewed: **Doctor Who** Series 5 – Brighter
Than Sunflowers.' *The Doctor Who Companion*, 21 December 2019.
https://thedoctorwhocompanion.com/2019/12/21/reviewed-
doctor-who-series-5-brighter-than-sunflowers/. Accessed 21
December 2019.

Cain, Fraser, 'Why Is Andromeda Coming Towards Us?' *Universe Today*, 22 January 2015. https://www.universetoday.com/118367/why-is-andromeda-coming-towards-us/. Accessed 20 January 2020.

Carroll, Sean, 'Ten Things Everyone Should Know About Time'. *Discover Magazine*, 1 September 2011. https://www.discovermagazine.com/the-sciences/ten-things-everyone-should-know-about-time. Accessed 25 November 2018.

Clark, Stuart, 'Starwatch: The Furthest Thing You Can See With The Naked Eye.' *The Guardian*, 25 August 2019. https://www.theguardian.com/science/2019/aug/25/starwatch-the-furthest-thing-you-can-see-with-the-naked-eye. Accessed 20 January 2020.

Cole, Tom, 'Steven Moffat: People Who Call **Sherlock** And **Doctor Who** Too Complex Are "Presumably Fairly Stupid".' *Radio Times*, 21 May 2012. https://www.radiotimes.com/news/2012-05-21/steven-moffat-people-who-call-sherlock-and-doctor-who-too-complex-are-presumably-fairly-stupid/. Accessed 21 December 2018.

Daley, Jason, 'Behold Hubble's Best Image Of A Distant Galaxy Yet.' *Smithsonian Magazine*, 19 January 2018. https://www.smithsonianmag.com/smart-news/hubble-captures-best-image-distant-galaxy-yet-180967862/. Accessed 18 May 2020.

Eck, Allison, 'Scientists Reverse Arrow of Time In Quantum Experiment.' *Nova*, 28 November 2017. https://www.pbs.org/wgbh/nova/article/scientists-reverse-arrow-of-time-in-quantum-experiment/. Accessed 24 November 2018.

Fernandes, Simon, 'Series 5, Episode 5: *Flesh and Stone.*' *Simon's*

Incoherent Blog, 4 May 2010.
https://blog.incoherent.net/2010/05/04/series-5-episode-5-flesh-and-stone/. Accessed 13 February 2020.

Fore, Meredith, 'Stephen Hawking Was Right: Black Holes Can Evaporate, Weird New Study Shows'. *Live Science*, 10 June 2019.
https://www.livescience.com/65683-sonic-black-hole-spews-hawking-radiation.html. Accessed 19 January 2020.

Fredsvenn, "'Sacred Marriage' Or 'Chaoskampf'". *Cradle of Civilization*, 28 July 2015.
https://aratta.wordpress.com/2015/07/28/on-the-chaoskampf/. Accessed 6 November 2018.

Fuller, Gavin, '**Doctor Who**: *The Pandorica Opens*'. *The Daily Telegraph*, 18 June 2010. Accessed 9 May 2020.

Fullerton, Huw, 'Is **Doctor Who** changing the rules of time travel?' *Radio Times*, 13 January 2020.
https://www.radiotimes.com/news/tv/2020-01-13/doctor-who-time-travel-rules/. Accessed 13 January 2020.

Fullerton, Huw, 'John Barrowman Responds To **Doctor Who**'s Sneaky Captain Jack Easter Egg'. *Radio Times*, 22 October 2018.
https://www.radiotimes.com/news/tv/2018-10-22/john-barrowman-responds-to-doctor-whos-sneaky-captain-jack-easter-egg/. Accessed 1 February 2020.

Fullerton, Huw, 'Steven Moffat Says **Doctor Who** Is The Perfect Escapism In Troubled Times: "It's A World Of Certainties Where Kindness And Tolerance Always Work Out".' *Radio Times*, 8 April 2020. https://www.radiotimes.com/news/tv/2020-04-08/steven-moffat-doctor-who-escapism/. Accessed 15 April 2020.

Gabbatiss, Josh, 'Most Distant Star Ever Seen Spotted By Hubble Telescope 9 Billion Light Years Away.' *The Independent*, 2 April 2018. https://www.independent.co.uk/news/science/star-light-years-galaxy-most-distant-ever-hubble-telescope-space-berkeley-a8284846.html. Accessed 1 June 2018.

Gaiman, Neil, Twitter, 11 April 2020. https://twitter.com/neilhimself/status/1249059895858663424. Accessed 17 April 2020.

Gaiman, Neil, 'Where Do You Get Your Ideas?' *NeilGaiman.com*, 1997. https://www.neilgaiman.com/Cool_Stuff/Essays/Essays_By_Neil/Where_do_you_get_your_ideas%3F. Accessed 3 February 2020.

Ghose, Tia, 'How To Teleport Info Out Of A Black Hole'. *Live Science*, 6 January 2016. https://www.livescience.com/53274-quantum-information-retrieval-black-hole.html. Accessed 21 January 2020.

Gill, NS, 'Hesiod's Five Ages of Man'. *Thought Co.*, updated 29 October 2019. https://www.thoughtco.com/the-five-ages-of-man-111776. Accessed 30 January 2020.

Gokturk, 'Elements Found In Fairy Tales'. *Ms Gokturk's Stuff*, 20 May 2008. http://www.surfturk.com/mythology/fairytaleelements.html. Accessed 5 November 2018.

Greene, Brian, 'Ask Brian Greene: What Exactly is the Universe Expanding Into?' *World Science Festival*, November 2011. https://www.worldsciencefestival.com/2011/11/ask_brian_green_what_is_the_universe_expanding_into/. Accessed 13 December

2018.

Hawking, Stephen, 'How To Build A Time Machine.' *The Daily Mail*, 27 April 2010. https://www.dailymail.co.uk/home/moslive/article-1269288/STEPHEN-HAWKING-How-build-time-machine.html. Accessed 25 November 2018.

Hesiod, 'Theogony'. *Michigan State University*. https://msu.edu/~tyrrell/theogon.pdf. Accessed 5 November 2018.

Jefferies, Lewis, 'Matt Smith's Debut **"Doctor Who"** Episode Was Based On Moffat's Childhood Dream.' *Futurism*, 2019. https://vocal.media/futurism/matt-smith-s-debut-doctor-who-episode-was-based-on-moffat-s-childhood-dream. Accessed 13 February 2020.

Jeffery, Morgan, 'All 11 series of **Doctor Who** ranked – from 2005 to 2018.' *Digital Spy*, 21 December 2018. https://www.digitalspy.com/tv/cult/a776343/doctor-who-series-ranked/. Accessed 22 December 2018.

Jones, Paul, 'Steven Moffat: The Companion Is The Main Character In **Doctor Who**, Not The Doctor.' *Radio Times*, 19 April 2012. https://www.radiotimes.com/news/2012-04-19/steven-moffat-the-companion-is-the-main-character-in-doctor-who-not-the-doctor/. Accessed 22 December 2018.

Kantey, Jordan, 'Writing Scene Breaks And Transitions That Develop Your Story.' *Now Novel*, 20 December 2018. https://www.nownovel.com/blog/writing-scene-breaks-transitions. Accessed 18 August 2019.

Kilson, Kashann, 'Dr. Who And The Bootstrap Paradox Is Sci-Fi Time Travel With Actual Physics.' *Inverse*, 14 October 2015.

https://www.inverse.com/article/7004-dr-who-and-the-bootstrap-paradox-is-sci-fi-time-travel-with-actual-physics. Accessed 26 November 2018.

MacDonald, Jessica, 'Weather In Egypt: Climate, Seasons, And Average Monthly Temperature.' *TripSavvy*, updated 3 June 2019. https://www.tripsavvy.com/egypt-weather-and-average-temperatures-4083354. Accessed 2 February 2020.

Maddox, Twitter, 5 February 2020. https://twitter.com/MaddoxProTweets/status/1225178680575627270. Accessed 15 April 2020.

Martin, Dan, 'Has **Doctor Who** Got Too Complicated?' *The Guardian*, 20 September 2011. https://www.theguardian.com/tv-and-radio/tvandradioblog/2011/sep/20/doctor-who-too-complicated. Accessed 17 August 2019.

Maleski, Sam, 'Tiberian Thoughts – The Woman And The Trap: Who And The Myth Of Pandora.' *DoWntime*, 5 November 2017. https://downtime2017.wordpress.com/2017/11/05/tiberian-thoughts-the-woman-and-the-trap-who-and-the-myth-of-pandora/. Accessed 12 November 2018.

McLean, Gareth, 'Steven Moffat: The Man With a Monster of a Job.' *The Guardian*, 22 March 2010. https://www.theguardian.com/media/2010/mar/22/stephen-moffat-doctor-who. Accessed 6 November 2018.

Micadei, Kaonan, John P.S. Peterson, et al., 'Reversing The Direction Of Heat Flow In Quantum Correlations.' *Cornell University*, 9 November 2017. https://arxiv.org/abs/1711.03323. Accessed 5 November 2018.

Miller, Cole, 'Black Holes And Neutron Stars.' *Department of Astronomy and Astrophysics, University of Chicago*, Unknown date. https://www.astro.umd.edu/~miller/poster1.html. Accessed 19 January 2020.

Mueller, Jennifer, 'Where Is The Warmest Climate Penguins Live?' *Mom.com*, unknown date. https://animals.mom.me/warmest-climate-penguin-lives-2850.html. Accessed 8 May 2020.

Mulkern, Patrick, 'Steven Moffat On His Early Years, Overcoming His Shyness, And The Pressures Of Running **Doctor Who** And **Sherlock**'. *Radio Times*, 30 November 2015. https://www.radiotimes.com/news/2015-11-30/steven-moffat-on-his-early-years-overcoming-his-shyness-and-the-pressures-of-running-doctor-who-and-sherlock/. Accessed 6 November 2018.

Novak, BJ, 'The Man Who Invented The Calendar.' *The New Yorker*, 28 October 2013. https://www.newyorker.com/magazine/2013/11/04/the-man-who-invented-the-calendar. Accessed 8 November 2018.

Pappas, Stephanie, 'Faster-Than-Light Discovery Raises Prospect Of Time Travel.' *Live Science*, 23 September 2011. https://www.livescience.com/16207-faster-light-discovery-time-travel.html. Accessed 26 November 2018.

Reynolds, Andrew, 'Steven Moffat Thought He May Leave **Doctor Who** In 2015.' *The Doctor Who Companion*, 23 March 2017. https://thedoctorwhocompanion.com/2017/03/23/steven-moffat-thought-he-may-leave-doctor-who-in-2015/. Accessed 13 February 2020.

Sharp, Tim, 'Alpha Centauri: Closest Star To Earth'. *Space.com*, 19

January 2018. https://www.space.com/18090-alpha-centauri-nearest-star-system.html. Accessed 20 January 2020.

Pickrell, John, 'Timeline: Human Evolution.' *New Scientist*, 4 September 2006. https://www.newscientist.com/article/dn9989-timeline-human-evolution/. Accessed 13 February 2019.

Rampton, James, '**Doctor Who**'s Steven Moffat On Why The Series Is Really A Kids' Programme.' *Stuff.Co.Nz*, 19 May 2017. https://www.stuff.co.nz/entertainment/tv-radio/92675373/doctor-whos-steven-moffat-on-why-the-series-is-really-a-kids-programme. Accessed 17 August 2019.

Redd, Nola Taylor, 'How Fast Does Light Travel? | The Speed of Light.' *Space.com*, 7 March 2018. https://www.space.com/15830-light-speed.html. Accessed 13 February 2019.

Riordan, Kate, 'How Setting Can Create Tension.' *Writers & Artists: The Insider Guide to the Media*, unknown date. https://www.writersandartists.co.uk/writers/advice/783/a-writers-toolkit/story-and-plot/. Accessed 7 January 2020.

Robinson, Joanna, 'Can The Man Behind **Sherlock** And **Doctor Who** Be Saved From Himself?' *Vanity Fair,* 10 July 2015. https://www.vanityfair.com/hollywood/2015/07/sherlock-doctor-who-steven-moffat-comic-con. Accessed 21 December 2018.

Rose, Frank, 'The Art of Immersion: Why Do We Tell Stories?' *Wired*, 8 March 2011. https://www.wired.com/2011/03/why-do-we-tell-stories/. Accessed 6 November 2018.

Siegel, Ethan, 'Earth Is Drifting Away From The Sun, And So Are All The Planets.' *Forbes*, 3 January 2019. https://www.forbes.com/sites/startswithabang/2019/01/03/earth-is-drifting-away-from-the-sun-and-so-are-all-the-planets/#5dc7a0b36f7d. Accessed 20 January 2020.

Southall, JR, 'From the Archives: **Doctor Who** *The Pandorica Opens / The Big Bang.*' *Starburst*, 24 August 2011. https://www.starburstmagazine.com/reviews/from-the-archive-the-pandorica-opens-the-big-bang Accessed 9 May 2020.

Than, Ker, 'Is Dark Energy Really "Repulsive Gravity"?' *National Geographic*, 16 February 2012. https://www.nationalgeographic.com/news/2012/2/120215-dark-energy-antimatter-physics-alternate-space-science/. Accessed 8 May 2020.

Traynier, David, 'First Ever Image of a Black Hole: *The Impossible Planet* Team Got It Right.' *The Doctor Who Companion*, 12 April 2019. https://thedoctorwhocompanion.com/2019/04/12/first-ever-image-of-a-black-hole-the-impossible-planet-team-got-it-right/. Accessed 14 April 2019.

University of Delaware, 'Penguin Population Could Drop 60 Percent By End Of The Century: Temperature Warming May Have Reached A Tipping Point.' *ScienceDaily*, 29 June 2016. www.sciencedaily.com/releases/2016/06/160629094848.htm. Accessed 2 February 2020.

Wilson, Glynn, 'Nature Abhors A Vacuum: From Aristotle To Thoreau'. *New American Journal*, 14 July 2019. https://www.newamericanjournal.net/2019/07/nature-abhors-a-vacuum-from-aristotle-to-thoreau/. Accessed 19 January 2020.

ACKNOWLEDGEMENTS

This is my first book, so of course, I need to thank everyone who has supported my writing so far, including (but certainly not limited to): Mum, Dad, Paul, Kay, Ian, Joan, Ruth, Sheila, Uncle Chris and Aunty Sonia, Christian Cawley, Mrs Millier, Mr Lewis, Mr Houghton, Marc Leverton, Julian Kendell, Claire Huxham, and Nick Abadzis.

A special thanks to my family who read everything I do, sometimes without bribery.

Thank you to Stuart Douglas and Philip Purser-Hallard for giving me this wonderful opportunity; to James Baldock, for polishing a particularly headache-inducing chapter (with my favourite bit of constructive feedback: 'This is retcon b*llocks and you know it'); to Scott Varnham, for tracking down that elusive issue of DWM; and to my editor, Paul Simpson, who has made this a lovely experience, been very generous with his time, and deleted all my type-ohs.

I'm also hugely grateful to the late Stan Lee for teaching me the value of stories, to Russell T Davies (you can probably guess why), and to Steven Moffat, who is something of a writing inspiration.

And thanks to you, too – thank you for picking up this book and so for supporting my general witterings. I really hope you've enjoyed it. This also covers me in case anyone moans they're not mentioned in the acknowledgements.

BIOGRAPHY

Philip Bates is the editor and co-founder of *The Doctor Who Companion*, so has been lucky enough to interview Matt Smith, Mark Strickson, and Mike Tucker (plus some lovely folk whose names don't begin with 'M'). He's also written for *MakeUseOf*, *The British Comedy Guide*, and *Hero Collector*.

His upcoming projects include *The Silver Archive: The Stone Tape* for Obverse Books, material for Lovarzi's **Doctor Who** and **Star Trek** ranges, and *100 Objects of Doctor Who* for Candy Jar.

He tried fish fingers and custard once. It was surprisingly nice.